Bastogne: Band of

Brothers Guide

Robert R. Allen

ISBN-13: 978-0-692-64783-7

DEDICATION

I'd like to dedicate this book to my mother. Although she's no longer with me her love and support will always be a source of strength.

Contents

List of Illustrations

Robert R. Allen

List of Maps

Robert R. Allen

Forward

I'll open this foreword with a question. What is a good guide book? In some cases a good guide book is almost as good as having a good guide, but a good guide book written by a good guide is as good as it gets. To any tourist interested in the subject it is a veritable hive of useful information and sound advice. The enthusiasm with which the guide book is written is a wonderfully transferable asset that will jump out at you from every page. That's what you'll get with this book. It's overtly apparent that Bob enjoys the subject with a level of dedication and passion that warms the hearts of irascible military historians such as me. Because he knows that it isn't enough just to be acquainted with your subject matter. Someone who takes the time and extreme effort to research, assemble, and compile a volume such as this goes way above and beyond the call of duty. It's a labor of love and it has to be otherwise these things would never get written in the first place.

Bob has that level of dedication that immediately engages the reader and takes them on that journey with him. Retracing the steps of indomitable heroes whose deeds we can only marvel at. Unless you have a good guide book a wall is just a wall, a building is just a building and a forest is a collection of deciduous and evergreen trees with no perceivable identity, until you read what happened at that certain location. Then they are no longer inanimate stones or pines. Then they are witnesses to history. Then they are places that the men of Easy Company saw through different eyes while ducking the bombs and bullets of a powerful enemy. Then they come to life.

I have visited European battlefields for over twenty five years and there is nothing better than having a good literary companion to help find one's way around and understand the places described. Therefore I heartily endorse this book and the person responsible for writing it. So to return to my initial question, what is a good guide book? Answer. This is!

Martin King

Cultural Ambassador

History Channel Consultant

Author of 'Voices of the Bulge', 'The Tigers of Bastogne', L'infermiére Oubliée

Robert R. Allen

Robert R. Allen

Preface

I'm a tour guide who specializes in military history tours. I do tours as a part time job so I'm asked quite often why I put so much time and energy into researching my tours. The answer is very simple, I'm addicted to history. To put it simply, history is my drug of choice.

When people find out that I'm a military history tour guide one of the first questions I get asked is if I do tours to Bastogne. I say yes, of course, so the second question is almost always something about the Band of Brothers. I've been asked about where to go in Bastogne and how to get there while I was in Verdun, Malmedy, and as far away as Normandy. I decided it was time to write a guidebook that will cover the movements of Easy Company in Bastogne in more detail.

The Battle of the Bulge, and especially the Battle for Bastogne, has always been a very interesting subject for me. This is one of the reasons that the Bastogne tour was the first tour I did when I became a tour guide in 2010. I worked researching this book for over three years but you could really say that I started the research by reading accounts about the subject for years before going back to my high school days in the early 1970's. I have a very large collection of books and magazines at home on the subject. I also have way too many bookmarks in my web browser to keep straight.

Even though I've been studying the events in Bastogne for years the real impact of what happened and the conditions the men endured didn't really hit home until the first time I visited Bastogne.

My first visit to Bastogne was during last part of April when spring should have officially started. I was standing in the Bois Jacques, where Easy Company was dug in; trying to imagine how the men felt. To my amazement it started to snow, yes snow in April! This was a very eerie experience for me.

I've been back to Bastogne many times in the snow and other weather conditions but this first visit sticks in my mind. Thinking about what these brave men went through, not only with the Germans but with the horrid weather conditions, makes my life's "trials" seem extremely trivial.

I wrote this book to help others experience the sites in Bastogne without having to figure out where everything is like I had to do. I would have been lost then without the help of Marilyn Meis who runs the Hotel Melba. She was far more help in finding places than the people in the information center.

This book contains maps and detailed directions to get to the major museums, sites and memorials in and around Bastogne. The book is laid out so that the map that corresponds to the locations in the chapter is on the first page of the chapter with directions to each location also included within the chapter. I wanted to do this so the reader will have the map available while reading through the locations covered.

In addition to information specifically about the Battle for Bastogne I've also included additional information about Easy Company including a timeline for the unit from its formation to its deactivation. I wrote this book to be a one-stop-shop type resource for Easy Company enthusiasts as well as those who are just developing an interest in the company.

I decided to include information about the city of Bastogne and other military sites and memorials that do not pertain directly to Easy Company. I wanted to help the visitor get the most complete experience possible.

To this end, I have also included information about the Combat Command B of the 10th Armored Division. Although seemingly lost in history the contributions of this unit must not be forgotten. It is safe to say that without the determination and sacrifices made by this group of men the Germans would have beat the 101st Airborne Division to Bastogne.

Even though much of the interest in Bastogne these days seems to be about Easy Company I feel it's important to remember the contributions made by everyone who fought to defend the city. In Appendix 6 you will find a list of the major units that fought in Bastogne. There were also stragglers who were picked up and thrown together into what was known as Team SNAFU. Although these stragglers were from many different units and were shaken by the experience of the German onslaught they merged together to form an effective fighting force.

The last chapter of the book provides GPS coordinates for each of the sites as well as instructions on how to make maps using Google Maps. When planning your visit I would suggest you allow at least one full day for visiting Bastogne and the surrounding area.

I would like to take time to say thank you to my daughter for making me realize the first approach I took in presenting this material was entirely wrong. I hope I did a good job at presenting the material in the manner she suggested. If I was able to accomplish this goal then the book will be a great asset to anyone who visits Bastogne.

I would also like to thank my friend and fellow author and history enthusiast Martin King for his guidance and support. He also provided suggestions for resources for my research and introduced me to people who are sources of invaluable information, Cheers Mate!!!

Robert R. Allen

Acknowledgements

First, I'd like to thank Marilyn Meis who runs the Hotel Melba in Bastogne with her husband Yves Stalars. She was a source of unlimited information when I first started visiting the locations included in this book. I'd like to thank Reg Jans for his help through the years especially with finding things in and around Bastogne. I'd also like to say a huge thanks to Martin King. Without his guidance and support I would never have been able to complete this book. I don't want to forget my daughter, my biggest supporter and harshest critic. She's the one that keeps me in line with my writing projects.

Robert R. Allen

Introduction

Although this book is intended to be a guidebook of Bastogne and the surrounding area it is much more. In addition to helping you find the points-of-interest for the Battle for Bastogne and Easy Company there is also information about the city of Bastogne. There is also background information about events that led up to the battle and information about the overall battle which became known as "The Battle of the Bulge." This information not only points out the different sites and areas of the city it also gives you an idea of why the city was so important to both the Allies and the Germans.

First, to fully understand an event like Bastogne and the Battle of the Bulge it is important to understand the events that lead up to the battle.

Starting in late July 1944 there was a chain of events that played a direct role in contributing to the situation that existed in the Ardennes region in December 1944. This book will discuss the events leading up to the Ardennes Offensive and explain the impact they had on the breakdown that occurred in the initial stages of the offensive.

There are also firsthand accounts from the people who fought in the battle. It is important to understand the human perspective of the events because wars are not fought by tanks, trucks, and artillery, wars are fought by men. The men in Bastogne had almost a psychotic fear of letting their friends down. Their determination was further strengthened when they learned that the Germans were killing American POWs.

Since this is meant to be a guidebook there are maps and directions to help you find the key sites, memorials, and museums that are located in and around Bastogne. The importance of each location, site, memorial, or person will be discussed. There is also information about several of the key individuals involved.

You will also find information pertaining directly to Easy Company, 506th Parachute Infantry Regiment, 101st Airborne Division. The information includes timelines and training. There is also information about the formation of the unit, and common attributes that the men shared. There is also some information about what happened to some of the men after the war.

This book is meant to provide information that is helpful and interesting to people with a wide range of knowledge of the Battle of Bastogne. Anyone from those who know nothing about the battle and the area to those who are well versed in the events will find it helpful to have all this information compiled together into one book.

Robert R. Allen

Robert R. Allen

Prologue

This engagement is known by several different names. The Americans call it the Battle of the Bulge, many simply call it the Ardennes Offensive, and the Germans know it as Wacht am Rhein. No matter what name you choose it is one of the most famous battles in history. It was a battle that took the ordinary American GI and turned him into a superhero in the eyes of the American public.

To completely understand the events during the Battle of the Bulge, especially the complete collapses that occurred during the opening stages of the engagement, it is important to understand what happened prior to the battle. The events that resulted in a battered, under strength force being in the Ardennes region go all the way back to August and the breakout from the Normandy beachheads.

The opening stages of Operation Cobra on July 25, 1944 signaled the breakout of the allied armies from Normandy. Over the next six weeks the Allies advanced to a point they did not expect to reach until the following spring. Field Marshal Montgomery's 21st Army Group encountered only minimal resistance during its advance toward Germany resulting in the Allies believing that the Germans were all but defeated. This would prove to be an extremely costly assumption.

The lack of resistance caused the normally cautious and extremely reserved Montgomery to quickly throw together what was to be the largest airborne operation in history to that point; Operation Market Garden. The operation was originally planned as a push by the British XXX Corps alone into Germany.

It was quickly realized that airborne support was needed for the operation to succeed. The American paratroops would jump into Holland to take and hold the bridges near Eindhoven and Nijmegen. The British airborne would use gliders to take and hold the final bridge at Arnhem. All the bridges needed to be captured and held for the operation to succeed. The operation was essentially doomed from the beginning.

The failure of Market Garden left the Americans with only the 2 corps in the Aachen area where there was still heavy fighting. It also meant there was only one corps that was stretched almost 90 miles to the south to protect the American front from Aachen to where Lt Gen Patton's 3rd Army was located on the southern flank.

To put this into perspective, imagine a medium sized corps of 30,000 stretched along a front 85-90 miles wide. This scenario means that if the men dug foxholes each would be about 16 feet apart making an effective defense almost impossible.

Unfortunately, this was the major portion of the defenses tasked with keeping contact with the Montgomery's 21st Army Group in the north and Patton's 3rd Army in the south.

In addition to the failure of Market Garden there was a second, maybe even more significant event that directly influenced the ability of the Allies, especially the Americans, to defend the Ardennes region; The Battle of the Hurtgen Forest. This area, known as the Schnee Eifel by the Germans, is in the northwest region of Germany near the Dutch border. The operation was originally initiated to take pressure off the fighting in the Aachen Pocket to the northwest but developed into a meat grinder claiming 33,000 American casualties.

The casualty rate was so high because the American leaders slipped back into a World War I mentality. They essentially opted to throw in more men in an attempt to make minimal gains on the ground. They were essentially trading off lives to advance just a few feet. The weather and harsh conditions in the forest also played a huge role in the causality level.

The fighting in this engagement was devastating to the units involved resulting in several infantry divisions being removed from fighting because they were completely devastated. Men from the 1st Infantry Division who fought on Omaha

Beach on D-Day said the fighting here was worse than on the beach. These depleted divisions along with newly formed units that never experienced combat were placed in the Ardennes to defend the area. None of the units in the Ardennes was in any shape to stop the German advance. This was supposed to be a quiet time for taking in replacements, training, and recuperation.

The offensive was the brainchild of Adolph Hitler as a way to swing the momentum of the war back to the German's advantage. During a meeting in the Wolf's Lair in September 1944 he suddenly lit up, slammed his hand on the map on the table and announced his intent to strike back at the allied forces that were rapidly approaching Germany. He intended to not only retake the important deep water port of Antwerp but also to fracture the fragile alliance between the Americans and the British.

Hitler hoped that by literally splitting the allies with his drive through Belgium both the English and Americans would start blaming the other for the failure in the Ardennes. He hoped this would cause distrust and result in the alliance breaking down. Hitler felt neither member of the alliance could stand alone against him and both sides would sue for peace. With England and America out of the war he could shift his attention to Russia where he desperately needed his forces.

The success of the operation depended on weather, secrecy, and speed. They needed bad weather to keep the allied planes on the ground thus negating the allied air superiority. They needed secrecy so the allies would not re-enforce the front in the Ardennes area. They also needed speed to reach their objectives before the weather broke which would allow the allies to provide close air support for the troops on the ground. They also needed to reach their objectives before the allies could regroup and launch a counterattack or deploy reinforcements to the area.

Probably the most important element to Hitler's plan was secrecy. In an attempt to ensure secrecy only the planners of the operation knew about Hitler's scheme until the time came when it was necessary to tell the senior military leaders. Strict radio silence was observed during the buildup for the offensive but the Allies were still able to figure out that something was going on across the Our River.

The men along the line heard tanks, armored vehicles, and other movement just across the river. There were reports from both GIs and civilians about the buildup of manpower and vehicles. There were even reports from Germans who were captured or surrendered but the American leaders did not believe it was anything significant. Even though the Germans attacked through the Ardennes in the past the allied leaders just refused to believe it was possible. The reports of the buildup went all the way up to Lt Gen Omar Bradley, commander of the 12th Army Group, who dismissed them. The allied commanders were convinced that any buildup was strictly a defensive move. The movement of troops and vehicles was carried out in a way so it looked like a defensive buildup in an attempt to fool the Allied leaders and it worked.

Operation Wacht am Rhein was a three-pronged offensive. The objective of the northern and central prongs of the attack was to push through the American defenses across the Meuse River and continue on to Antwerp. This would give Germany the deep water port it so desperately needed to bring in supplies and raw materials. The southern prong was intended to cover the 5th Panzer Armee's left flank defending it against General Patton's 3rd Army which was sure to become involved in the battle from the south.

General Joseph "Sepp" Dietrich was in command the 6th SS Panzer Armee in the north. His 1st SS Panzer Division, commanded by Lt Col Jochen Peiper, was the spearhead of the attack tasked with crossing the Meuse River at Huy.

General of the Panzer Armee Hasso von Manteuffel was in command of the 5th Panzer Armee in the center, which became known as the Bastogne

Corridor. His 2nd Panzer Division, commanded by Lt Gen Meinard von Lauchert, was the spearhead of the attack tasked with crossing the Meuse River at Dinant. This was quite a task especially since von Lauchert did not assume command of the division until the night before the attack began.

The 2nd Panzer Division succeeded in getting closer to the Meuse River than any other German unit. They reached their deepest point in the bulge on December 25, 1944. They were able to advance a total of approximately 95 kilometers (60 miles) into the allied line before being stopped. They were finally stopped at Celles which is only about 4 kilometers (3 miles) from the bridge in Dinant and the Meuse River.

The advance was halted by a combined force made up of the British 29th Armored Brigade and the American 2nd Armored Division. There are stories that a small portion of Col Otto Skorzeny's unsuccessful Operation Grief, special commando group which was assigned to Lt Col Peiper's unit, was able to make it across the bridge at Dinant. Even if this was true the group was too small to have any effect on the outcome of the offensive. However; the fact that enemy troops were in the American lines posing as Americans caused a lot of concern. Gen Eisenhower's security staff increased security and controlled his actions more closely. It was feared this group's assignment was to assassinate Eisenhower. All the extra security only proved to irritate Eisenhower.

After being stopped the 2nd Panzer Division fought a continual rearguard action until the unit was almost completely wiped out. By the end of the fighting the unit essentially ended up being just a mark on the map. What was left of the 2nd Panzer Division ended up trapped on the west bank of Rhein River with no way to cross. Lt Gen von Lauchert swam across the river with some of his staff members to evade capture. He was so fed up with the war he walked around 250 kilometers (155 miles) back to Bamberg.

General Erich Brandenberg in command of the all infantry 7th Armee advanced on the southernmost flank of the offensive. The main objective of this unit was to protect von Manteuffel's left flank. The 7th Armee units were undermanned and did not have the normal complement of artillery, mortars, and assault guns that usually made up an infantry unit. Because of the lack of vehicles the unit also had to rely heavily on horses to pull the few artillery pieces and assault guns that were available.

The offensive was planned to push into Belgium and Luxembourg in a manner similar to the attack that took place on May 10, 1940. One of the main differences was the attack in December 1944 would be required to advance against the established roadways instead of with them. Once the offensive pushed through the Ardennes it was to advance toward the deep-water port at Antwerp. The goal of the 6th SS Panzer Armee was the bridge across the Meuse River at Huy. The 5th Panzer Armee was assigned to cross the Meuse at Dinant. The Germans needed to reach these objectives before the Americans could destroy the bridges.

General von Manteuffel's original plan did not include the capture of Bastogne. It was basic German tactics since the Franco/Prussian war of 1870-1871 to bypass strongholds to reach planned objectives more quickly. The idea was that the main spearhead of the advance would pass by and leave the rear units to capture the strongholds at a later time.

General von Manteuffel's plan was no different in this respect. His plan called for the 2nd Panzer Division and the Panzer Lehr to go around Bastogne to the north and push on to the Meuse River. He would leave the 26th Volksgrenadier (VG) in the rear for a type of mop up action. Von Manteuffel didn't expect much resistance from the units in Bastogne. At the time the offensive began Bastogne was being used as the headquarters for Maj Gen Troy Middleton's VIII Corps and had very few real combat troops.

However; as soon as Gen von Manteuffel learned that that an airborne division was heading to Bastogne to hold the city he had to adjust his plans. He knew the 26th VG would not be able to capture Bastogne alone against such an elite fighting force. As a result von Manteuffel was forced to leave the Panzer Lehr to help out. The loss of the armored unit meant his spearhead pushing toward the Meuse River was weakened.

The 82nd Airborne Division was actually supposed to go to Bastogne in the beginning. The unit was able to mobilize and get on the road before the 101st Airborne Division. Because of this it was decided to send them to Werbomont on the northern shoulder instead where the defenders desperately needed help in stopping Kampfgruppe Pieper's advance. BG McAuliffe did not know about this change and left Mourmelon planning on leading his unit to Werbomont.

BG McAuliffe decided to stop at Bastogne to talk directly to Maj Gen Troy Middleton, the commander of the VIII Corps, on his way to get more details about the situation. When he met with Maj Gen Middleton he was informed that the 101st Airborne Division would be going to Bastogne instead of Werbomont.

The combination of the weakening of the units from the Hurtgen Forest and the lack of training and experience of the new units meant the units defending the Ardennes region didn't have a chance against the push of a force of approximately 250,000. The Americans were outnumbered roughly 3 to 1. To add to the confusion the Germans were able to penetrate American lines and cut many of the phone lines. They also knew the radio frequencies we used and jammed them with continual music broadcasts. These two factors made any kind of communications almost impossible.

The force that attacked Bastogne outnumbered the Americans by roughly 2 to 1. The main body of the force was made up of the 26th Volksgrenadier (people's infantry), 5th Parachute Division, the Panzer Lehr, and the 2nd Panzer Division.

The Volksgrenadier units were made up of people who were previously deemed unfit for duty for a number of different reasons. They were originally too old or young or possibly had some type of physical condition that prevented them from serving. There were also select groups in jobs that were classified as essential to the war effort who were exempt from military service.

However; by this point in the war Germany was desperate for soldiers and waived most age and physical restrictions. Many of the individuals who were exempt because of their jobs found themselves on the front line because the raw materials weren't available to keep the factories productive.

The Germans were also moving people from other branches of service and every imaginable job in the military into the infantry. The Luftwaffe (Air Force) and Kriegsmarine (Navy) were all but obsolete by this point in the war so large numbers of the men were transferred to the infantry as well. The Wehrmacht (Army) also started counting more on conscripts from the countries that Germany now controlled. There were many cases of these men surrendering because they felt no obligation to risk their lives for Germany.

The result of all the changes in policy would have consequences. There were many of the men who fought in the Ardennes who never held a rifle. These men were cooks, bakers, clerks, and many other specialties with no formal combat training.

The idea of creating this large influx of men, although not combat trained, was to pour as many men as possible into the offensive as quickly as possible to shock the Americans. It was meant to overpower the defenses buy sheer numbers. It did not always work to the German's advantage. There are many stories about American soldiers encountering Germans who were just standing there not knowing what to do or entering into the battle standing upright with no idea of how to pick their targets before firing.

In some areas the Americans were outnumbered 10-1 but still held the line. At first this could be credited to the fact that the Germans still didn't have their tanks or support guns over the Our River but the lack of training also played a huge role. The officers and experienced NCOs had to try to urge the men on in battle from the front and were soon killed. The remaining men didn't know how to recognize or press an advantage when it presented itself.

Some of the attacking force was very well trained. The Panzer Lehr, for example, was made up of the instructors who taught the panzer crews and demonstration teams. These crews were highly skilled and knew armored battle tactics and strategy like it was second nature. They were brought into service after it was realized that keeping these highly trained individuals out of the fight was no longer a choice. Besides, the construction of new tanks and the formation of new crews had almost ceased so it was no longer necessary to have tank training schools.

The conditions in Bastogne were dire. The locals feared being once again forced under the brutal hand of Nazi control. The town had just been liberated on September 16, 1944 after over 4 years of occupation and they hadn't even gotten used to life without the Germans when the town was attacked and surrounded. It looked to everyone like the German occupation was about to begin again.

The reoccupation of the city not only meant that the people would once again be under German control it also meant far worse for some of the less fortunate. Anyone who was "guilty" of helping the Americans would be executed. There would be more than enough people who were willing to point out anyone who helped the Americans in an attempt to make their own life easier. The outlook for the city was very grim.

The conditions on the front were made worse by the lack of supplies making it from the Normandy beaches and Cherbourg to the front. The port at Antwerp, although captured in September 1944, wasn't usable until the entrance to the port along Scheldt estuary coming from the English Channel was opened. The allies were not able to secure the estuary until long after Antwerp was originally taken. The first large ships weren't able to start using the port till November 28, 1944. Even after the port at Antwerp was opened it was never used to its full capacity.

The men went into combat wearing what they had on when they were notified to move to the front. The men who were on passes were loaded into open top trucks in their dress uniforms. There were no seats in the trucks so they had to stand or sit on the floor the entire trip. Some had wool overcoats but many had the normal jump uniform and boots. This type of uniform offered little help in keeping the men warm. To make matters worse, the winter of 1944-1945 was the coldest on record up till that time with temperatures dropping to -28 Celsius at night.

The men who were already in the Ardennes weren't much better off. The decision not to issue cold weather gear was made by the Quarter Masters in August leaving the men ill equipped. They opted to ship only fuel and ammunition to the front since nobody expected any action in the area. They probably weren't expecting the harsh winter that was about to hit the area that necessitated the warm clothing even without the attack.

The lack of proper clothing was overcome by the imagination of the troops. They learned what hobos and homeless people have known for years. They started packing paper between their skin and clothes. They also learned to dry their wet socks in the armpits and crotches.

Some learned that if they held hands and pushed up against trees and rotated around the tree to create friction it would help to keep them warm. If their foxhole was big enough they would sleep three to a foxhole. They would rotate sleeping positions so each man would have time in the middle thus taking advantage of the body heat of the other two to stay warm.

The lack of a deep water port closer to the front meant that supplies needed to be transported via truck. This is where the famous "Red Ball Express" came into play. This supply chain ran 24 hours a day 7 days a week in an attempt to keep the frontline troops supplied. But even this herculean effort couldn't make up for all the problems in the supply chain.

The biggest problem was that it was a chain. The supply requests passed through many offices at many levels before being approved and the shipments were made. There were several stops along the route of the Red Ball Express with differing levels of brass at each stop. Much of the equipment and food needed by the frontline troops was diverted at the rear by people who didn't really need it.

As bad as this was there was another drain on the supplies going to the front; the black market. It was common for people to take advantage of the supplies flowing to the front to use them for personal gain.

Both of these issues meant that much of the equipment that should have gone to the frontline troops never made it past the rear echelons. In normal circumstances this was bad; in the case of Bastogne and the other locations in the bulge it was devastating. For example, at one point in Bastogne the artillery pieces were down to 1 or 2 rounds and the men were down to just a few rounds for their rifles. This meant they were extremely restricted in their ability to defend the city.

The loss of supplies meant that even when the C-47s were able to get through to Bastogne the supplies were only enough to hold them for another couple of days. This is partly because some of the C-47s never made to the drop zone.

The challenges for the men fighting in Belgium were compounded by the fact that the Germans weren't the only force against them. This area of Belgium changed hands so many times through the years before the war that there were still many Belgians who considered themselves to be German. These people aided the Germans by pointing out where American forces were and where individuals were hiding. They also took up arms and killed many of the men.

When the 101st Airborne Division arrived in Bastogne there was also an issue about who would be in command of the two distinct units. The 10th Armored Division was already in Bastogne and its commander Col William L. Roberts felt like he should retain command of his unit. He, like many armored commanders, did not like the fact that the infantry considered tanks as mobile forts or pillboxes.

Maj Gen Troy Middleton, commander of the VIII corps understood the colonel's concerns but he also understood the importance of unity of command so he put BG McAuliffe in overall command. The idea of being under the control of the infantry left the armored units a little apprehensive but all they could do is hope that BG McAuliffe would know how to use the armored assets appropriately.

To ensure armored firepower was available where needed BG McAuliffe assembled his available artillery into three mobile fire teams to quickly meet any attack made by the Germans. These mobile fire teams were so effective that the Germans thought there was much more firepower in Bastogne than was really there.

The Germans aided in the illusion by only attacking at single points around the perimeter looking for a soft spot for a break through. This allowed the fire teams to concentrate their full efforts into small areas making their defenses seem much more formidable.

The final situation in Bastogne was set when the 101st Airborne Division arrived in Bastogne. The first action taken by BG McAuliffe was to send the 1st Battalion from the 506th PIR to Noville to reinforce Maj Desobry's team. The valiant stand of Team Desobry and men from the 101st Airborne Division came at a high price. Maj Desobry was wounded when a soldier parked a vehicle in front of Desobry's command post, something that should not be done. The Germans fired on the building reasoning it was the command post. Maj Desobry was severly wounded and was lost for the rest of the war when he was captured with the 101st Airborne Division's entire hospital staff.

The 101st Airborne Division also lost the commander of the 1st Battalion, 506th PIR in the same incident. Lt Col James L. LaPrade was in the command post with Maj Desobry when it was attacked. The poor judgment and failure to follow protocol of one man resulted in the loss of two valuable commanders almost before the fight began.

The second action by McAuliffe was to send the 501st PIR to the southern side of Bastogne to assist Team Cherry in the Mageret, Neffe, Mont area. The combined forces were able to stop the advance of the Panzer Lehr commanded by Gen Fritz Bayerlein. Team Cherry was absorbed into the line of the 501st PIR in the area near the town of Mont and that portion of the perimeter was set.

It should be pointed out that Gen McAuliffe almost did not make it back to Bastogne before the city was surrounded. He went to see Maj Gen Middleton at his new command post in Neufchateau, which is southwest of Bastogne, to discuss the situation in Bastogne. He barely made it back to

Bastogne before the Germans were successful in encircling the city. The only route left open just happened to be in the southwest, the direction from which McAuliffe arrived.

Contact Information

101st Airborne Museum
Web Site:
http://www.101airbornemuseumbastogne.com/
E-mail: johnny.bona@mil.be

101st Airborne Command Post Bastogne Barracks
Web Site:
http://www.battleofthebulgememories.be/museums1
2/belgium11/825-bastogne-barracks-museum.html
E-mail: johnny.bona@mil.be

Bastogne War Museum
Web Site: http://www.bastognewarmuseum.be/uk-
bastogne-war-museum.html
E-mail: info@bastognewarmuseum.be

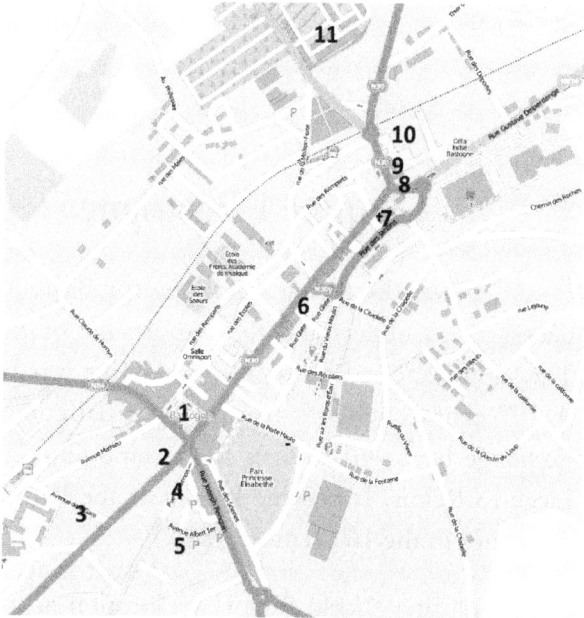

Bastogne Map Chapter 1

1. McAuliffe Square – Information Center, Tank, and McAuliffe Bust.
2. Plaque to Renee Lemaire
3. 101st Airborne Museum
4. Pays d' Ardennes Museum
5. Patton Memorial
6. Latin Quarter
7. St Peter's Church
8. WWI and WWII Memorial
9. I was 20 in 45 in Bastogne Expo
10. 101st Airborne Aid Station
11. 101st Airborne Command Post

Chapter 1 Bastogne

When discussing the Battle for Bastogne it is necessary to understand the importance of the city. The significance of Bastogne goes all the way back to the 9th century when it became a crucial commercial exchange between Brussels to Luxembourg City and Liege to Reims. It became known as the Paris of the Ardennes in the 16th century.

During World War II its location as a major crossroads city made it a strategic strong point for both the Allies and Germans. The side that controlled Bastogne controlled the flow of supplies and troops in the area. In addition to the roadways in and out of Bastogne there was also a railroad that passed through the city which made the movement of troops and large amounts of supplies possible.

All of the museums and memorials located in Bastogne are within easy walking distance with the furthest being about 15 minutes from the Information Center. You can park your car in the parking lot next to the Information Center. If you plan on staying in Bastogne I would recommend the Best Western Hotel Melba. The hotel is just down the road from McAuliffe Square on Avenue Mathieu making it convenient and it also has a private parking lot. They offer discounts to active duty and retired military if you make this known at the time of booking.

We begin the tour at the information center located in McAuliffe Square (1) located on Rue de Marche. The information center is the circular building located near the Sherman tank and bust of Brigadier General Anthony C. McAuliffe.

Figure 1 Bust of McAuliffe (From Author's Collection)

Brigadier General Anthony Clement McAuliffe was the commanding general in Bastogne during the Battle of the Bulge. He assumed command because the 101st Airborne Division commander Maj Gen Maxwell Taylor was in Washington D.C. testifying at a military hearing. BG McAuliffe was told by Maj Gen Troy Middleton, VIII Corps commander, to hold Bastogne at all costs. Maj Dick Winters later said that he felt McAuliffe being in command gave the 101st Airborne Division a fighting chance they would not have if Maj Gen Taylor were in command.

When McAuliffe joined the airborne he went through training as an artillery officer. Thanks to this training he was able to take full advantage of the artillery he had at his disposal. He understood the correct use of the artillery and the men trusted his decisions. His abilities and dogged dedication to duty impressed Hitler so much that he said he wished his generals were more like McAuliffe.

Even with his expert handling of the armored and artillery assets in Bastogne he is most famous for one simple word. His greatest claim to fame is for providing what is probably the most well known reply to a surrender request in history: NUTS!

McAuliffe actually seemed a little amused when he first received the surrender request from the Germans. His first response was "Us surrender? Aw, nuts."

He waited to respond to the surrender request until Col Kinnard, the 101st Airborne Division operations officer, pointed out that the time limit for the response was approaching. McAuliffe said he didn't know how to respond. Col Kinnard would later say that being a smart alec young colonel he of course told BG McAuliffe, "That first remark of yours would be hard to beat" and that's how the famous NUTS! reply was born.

When Gen von Lüttwitz, commander of the XLIX Corps was told that NUTS! basically meant "go to hell" he was not impressed. The bold reply enraged the Germans and lead to the bombing on Christmas Eve that killed Renee Lemaire who will be discussed later.

Although BG McAuliffe was in agreement that the 101st Airborne Division did not need to be "rescued" by Lt Gen Patton he was still uneasy with the fact that the 10th Armored Division didn't get the credit it deserved in the defense of the city especially with the press. In his book NUTS! Kenneth McAuliffe, the general's greatnephew, quoted BG McAuliffe as saying;

> *"It seems regrettable to me that Combat command B of the 10th Armored division didn't get the credit it deserved at the battle of Bastogne. All the newspaper and radio talk was about the paratroopers. Actually the 10th Armored division was in there a day before*

we were and had some very hard fighting before we ever got into it, and I sincerely believe that we would never have been able to get into Bastogne if it had not been for the defensive fighting of the three elements of the 10th Armored division who were first into Bastogne and protected the town from invasion by the Germans."

Even though the men of the 10th Armored Division did not get all the recognition they deserved, from by the press, they were recognized by the military. Combat Command B which supported the 101st Airborne Division also received the Presidential Unit Citation for its actions. The confusion was probably caused because the unit was under the command of BG McAuliffe while they were in Bastogne making it seem like it was completely a 101st Airborne Division defense of the town.

Figure 2 Sherman Tank on McAuliffe Square (From Author's Collection)

The Sherman tank known as "Barracuda" located at McAuliffe Square (1) was from the 11th Armored Division. The plaque on the left side as you're facing the tank reads:

IN HONOR
OF THE VALIANT MEN
OF THE 10th US ARMORED DIVISION
WHO GAVE THEIR LIVES FOR FREEDOM
IN THE 1944-1945 ARDENNES CAMPAIGN
AND IN THE BASTOGNE AREA

The plaque at the front of the tank reads:

This tank, knocked out in December 1944 recalls the sacrifice of all the fighters for the liberation of Bastogne and Belgium.

The 11th Armored Division first entered the battle on the morning of December 30, 1944. The unit attacked northerly from positions on the south flank. The unit attacked into the face of a simultaneous German counterattack intended to close the narrow corridor that had been opened into the Bastogne perimeter from the south.

Combat Command B of the 11th Armored successfully liberated the villages of Lavasalle and Houmont, but suffered significant casualties.

Early in the engagement, "Barracuda," under the command of Staff Sgt. Wallace Alexander, and a companion tank commanded by Captain Robert L. Ameno, became separated from the rest of the company. They moved north into enemy held terrain, approaching the village of Renuamont, the command post of Colonel Otto Ernst Remer, Kommandeur of Hitler's elite Führer Begleit Brigade. After being discovered by an astounded Col Remer himself, they came under attack.

"Barracuda," became bogged down in a snow covered pond while attempting break off from the engagement. Unable to maneuver it became a sitting duck for enemy tank and panzerfaust (a German hand-held anti-tank weapon) fire. Tank commander Staff Sgt. Wallace Alexander was mortally wounded; gunner Cpl Cecil Peterman and loader Pfc. Dage Herbert were wounded and captured. Driver Tech/4 Andrew Urda and Bow gunner Pfc. Ivan Goldstein were uninjured, but captured.

Although he survived the battle Alexander died several days later in captivity. Peterman and Herbert received minimal medical treatment for their wounds, survived, and were incarcerated as prisoners of war in Stalag XIIA near Limburg, Germany. Urda and Goldstein also eventually made it to Stalag XIIA, but only after being treated, not as prisoners of war, but as slave laborers.

Goldstein and Urda did not fare as well in captivity as Peterman and Herbert. Goldstein was identified as Hebrew by his dog tags, and by a letter in his pocket from his mother, reminding him to observe the Jewish holiday, Hanukkah. Goldstein and Urda had already made a pact, vowing to stay together in captivity. They narrowly escaped execution, but were brutally overworked and starved. After their liberation near the end of the war, the two severely emaciated captives spent many months recovering in US Army Hospitals.

In the end Andrew Urda never fully recovered from his mistreatment in captivity. He died in 1979 from health complication caused by his treatment as a POW. Ivan Goldstein's health was eventually restored. As of the printing of this book he lives in Jerusalem.

The other tank in the engagement commanded by Captain Ameno was also destroyed, killing him and four members of his crew. The fifth crewman was wounded and died in captivity a short time later.

The large white house across the street from the Information Center belonged to the Mathieu family. The family used to be horse breeders and held a very prominent position in the community. This house is mentioned because it draws a lot of attention since it stands out from the rest of the buildings in and around the square.

Figure 3 Mathieu Family (From Author's Collection)

After getting a map from the information center and getting pictures of the tank and McAuliffe memorial stand next to the information center with the building on your right and the road on your left. We will start this tour at the site of the former Hotel Le Brun. This is where Col Roberts, commander of CCB, 10th Armored Division, had his command post. Just walk straight down the road for about 120 meters. The building is hard to recognize now because the entire front of the building was changed.

Now turn around and face back in the direction you came from. You will see the traffic light that is just past the information center from where you started. Walk toward the traffic lights.

The next stop will be the plaque that is dedicated to Renee Lemaire (2) the nurse who was depicted in the mini-series Band of Brothers. Go to the corner where the traffic light is and turn right to cross over to the opposite side of Rue de Marche. The traffic light will be behind you and you will be on the right side of Rue de Neufchateau heading away from McAuliffe Square. At the time of this printing the plaque is located on the front of an Asian restaurant called the Cite Wok that is about 130 meters from the traffic light.

Figure 4 Plaque to Renee Lemaire (From Author's Collection)

The text on the plaque reads:

IN MEMORIAM
SITE OF THE AID STATION
OF THE 20th A.I.B. 10th
ARMORED DIVISION WHERE
OVER THIRTY U.S. WOUNDED
AND 1 VOLUNTEER BELGIAN
NURSE (RENEE LEMAIRE)
WRE INSTANTLY KILLED
BY A GERMAN BOMB
DECEMBER 24, 1944

Renee Bernadette Emilie Lemaire was born April 10, 1914 in Bastogne Belgium.

Renee was a registered nurse who worked in a hospital in Brussels and was home to visit her family for Christmas when the Germans attacked. She was trapped in Bastogne when the Germans encircled the town.

Most of the 101st Airborne's medical staff was either captured or killed when the divisional medical staff surrendered on December 19, 1944. As a result of the lack of medically qualified people to care for the wounded there was a request made for anyone willing and capable to aid with the casualties. Renee was more than happy to lend a hand.

She worked with the casualties from the 20th Armored Infantry Battalion of the 10th Armored Division in the Sarma Department store. The aid station had to be moved 2 times during the battle. It was first located in Noville when Team Desobry from Combat Command B was there trying to stop the German advance. It was moved to Rue du Vivier and then finally to the store on Route de Neufchateau.

Since Renee worked in the 10th Armored Division aid station not the 101st Airborne Division aid station most people feel it was not likely that she and Doc Eugene Roe from Easy Company ever met. There is a possibility they may have met while Doc Roe was scrounging for medical supplies but it's doubtful.

Renee began working on the December 21, 1944 when there were about 150 patients in the aid station; many of the men were seriously injured. At the time her main job was to change dressings and to assist those who could not clean or feed themselves.

It is said that she was not good with handling the blood and gore of the more serious cases but that's not where her strength resided. Her true value came from the effect she had on the men. Her presence seemed to be an inspiration to the men calming them and making them feel like they had a chance to survive. In serious cases sometimes just believing you will survive makes all the difference in the world.

She only served for 4 days before she was killed in the bombing that occurred on Christmas Eve. The circumstances surrounding her death are confusing to say the least. Capt Geiger form the 10th Armored Division reported that he saw Renee come out of the aid station after one bomb hit. She was helping the wounded escape calling for help and water indicating the building was on fire. He said she entered the building again and it was hit by a second bomb killing her instantly.

Another version says that Renee was in the kitchen of the aid station when the attack began. She either went into the basement or was pushed into the basement when the bombing began. When the bomb hit the aid station everyone else who remained in the kitchen was blown clear of the building because one wall of the building in the kitchen was glass. Renee was killed instantly with the other people in the basement.

Dr Prior, who was in command of the aid station and who was in the next room during the attack, said there was only one bomb that hit the aid station.

The state of Renee's remains when found is also not clear. Dr Prior and a journalist from Bastogne reported that only the top half of Renee's body was recovered from the rubble. Others, including Dr Prior in another report, simply said that

Renee's remains were found. Augusta Chiwy, Renee's friend, said that her body was found in two pieces.

The one thing that seems to be agreed on is that Dr Prior wrapped her remains in white parachute silk that Renee dearly wanted for a wedding dress and returned them to her parents for burial.

The important thing to remember about all this is that as far as the men of the 10th Armored Division are concerned the circumstances of her death and condition of her remains simply aren't important. To them what matters is the care she provided to the wounded and feeling of hope she gave them. Renee's presence calmed the men and gave them the will to live. To them she truly earned the title of "Angel of Bastogne". (See appendix 8 for Capt Prior's recommendation for recognition of Renee's contributions).

Renee was finally recognized for her sacrifices and service on December 10, 2010 when she posthumously awarded the Knight of the Order of the Crown. Since that day she is known as Lady Lemaire.

The following picture is a display in the NUTS! Cave BG McAuliffe's command post. There is a picture of Renee and the Knight of the Order of the Crown medal that was awarded to Renee. This award is normally reserved for members of the military or for civilians who have made significant contributions over a long period of service. This is the same medal that was awarded to Augusta Chiwy, who will be talked about next, almost 70 years after she served in Bastogne.

Figure 5 Knight of the Order of the Crown (From Author's Collection)

There is one very important person who was almost completely forgotten by history, Augusta Chiwy. She is the Congolese nurse who served at the 10th Armored Division aid station with Renee Lemaire. She finally received the recognition she deserves thanks to the work of Martin King, a fellow historian, who brought her story to life in his book "'L'infermiére Oubliée'" ("The Forgotten Nurse").

Augusta Chiwy was born in the Belgian Congo in 1921.

Augusta was a nurse at the St Elizabeth General Hospital in Louvain, Belgium. She was in Bastogne visiting her family for the Christmas holidays when the Germans surrounded the city. She arrived in Bastogne from Brussels about 1700 on December 17, 1944.

Augusta decided to go directly to her uncle's house first to get more information about the situation. Her dad Dr Chiwy had a small practice in the town so she when there next to see if she could help.

She was friends with Renee Lemaire and both remained in the safety of Augusta's uncle's basement until December 21, 1944 when they both decide to volunteer their help.

When she left her uncle's basement she immediately started assisting the wounded, both military and civilian. The 10th Armored Division medical staff was on the lookout for help and asked her to join them when they saw her. She began working with them that day.

Although her main duties were to assist the wounded in the aid station she was asked on at least one occasion by Dr Prior, who ran the aid station, to go with him to get the wounded from the front line.

She went with the rest of the team during a raging blizzard in a duce-and-a-half (truck) dressed in American military clothing because her clothes were drenched in blood by then. If captured her being in uniform would mean instant death. Although probably not even 5' tall and slight of build she assisted in putting the wounded into the trucks to be transported back to the aid station.

Augusta was in the building right next to the 10th Armored Division aid station with Dr Prior when the attack that killed Renee occurred. The blast blew her through a wall but she survived uninjured.

Augusta seemed to pass into history forgotten until Martin King decided to take up the cause of finding out what happened to this remarkable lady. He managed to locate her and she finally received the recognition she deserved. She received a letter of appreciation from the surviving members of the 10th Armored Division as well as a letter from King Albert II of Belgium recognizing her services.

On June 24, 2011 Augusta became Lady Chiwy when she was presented with the Knight of the Order of the Crown. When she was asked about the award she remarked that it took almost 70 years but it would make a good story to tell her grandchildren. Augusta still lives in Brussels.

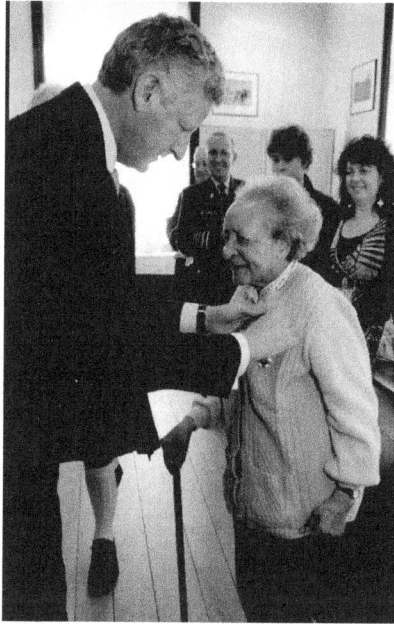

Figure 6 Lady Chiwy Receiving the Knight of the Order of the Crown Lady
(Courtesy of Martin King)

Now continue down the road to the next intersection and turn right onto Avenue de la Gare. Just down the road on the right is the 101st Airborne Division Museum. The museum is owned and run by Johnny Bona as of the printing of this book. You can contact him at e-mail: johnny.bona@mil.be for information about the museum as well as the Bastogne Barracks, mentioned later, where he is the commandant.

Figure 7 The 101st Airborne Museum (From Author's Collection)

The 101st Airborne Division Museum (3) just opened at the beginning of 2012. The displays are spread over 3 floors with a combination of show cases and dioramas. The owner is working on expanding the museum into the basement as of the printing of this book.

There is also a small gift shop on the first floor. When you go past the desk where you pay turn to your left. You will come to an area where there is a drink machine. The entrance to the gift shop is to the right of the drink machine.

While visiting the museum don't forget to have your picture taken with the Bastogne sign. It makes a very good souvenir of your visit. The person working in the museum will be more than happy to take the picture for you.

You can find more information about the 101st Airborne Museum at the following web site:

http://www.101airbornemuseumbastogne.com/

When you finish here exit the museum and turn left and return toward the center of the town in the direction you came. When you get to Rue de Neufchateau cross the road and turn left. Just down the street you will find the Musée du Pays (4). This museum is a combination of items collected after the Battle of the Bulge and a natural history museum. It is worth a quick look.

Figure 8 Pays d' Ardennes – The First Museum (From Author's Collection)

You can find more information about the museum at:

http://www.battleofthebulgememories.be/en/museu ms/belgium/236-au-pays-dardenne-original-museum-belgium.html

Now we will go to the Patton Memorial (5) which is located in a parking lot approximately 350 meters from this museum.

Turn right when you exit the museum and head back toward the traffic light in the center of town. At the traffic light turn right down Rue Joseph-Renquin. There is a large parking lot approximately 170 meters from the traffic light on the right side of the street. When you approach the parking lot you will see the Patton Memorial at the back of the parking lot.

Figure 9 Patton Memorial (From Author's Collection)

The memorial was erected to honor Lt Gen George Smith Patton Jr. for the part he played in breaking the siege at Bastogne on December 26, 1944. The siege ended when the Cobra King from the 4th Armored Division linked up with a member of the 101st Airborne Division engineers at a pillbox southwest of Bastogne.

Patton was able to break contact with the Germans and turn 4 of his divisions 90 degrees to race toward Bastogne. The tanks and armored vehicles ignored all blackout protocols to ensure they would reach Bastogne as quickly as possible. They covered over 100 miles against strong resistance in about 4 days.

There is a plaque to the left of the memorial at ground level. The plaque is facing toward the street. It is dedicated to the 11th Belgian Fusilier (light infantry). The plaque reads:

I desire to commend the 11th Belgian Fusilier Battalion for meritorious and outstanding performance of military duty while serving with the Third United States Army... Dwight D. Eisenhower Supreme Commander 13 July 1945

Now return to the traffic light at the corner by the information center. When you arrive at the light turn to the right to head toward the St Peter's church. You will now be going through what is known as the Latin Quarter (6) because of the Latin school that was located here which was founded by the Trinitarians who were in Bastogne since 1242.

Our next stop is at St Peter's Church (7), the church that is often misrepresented as the aid station of the 101st Airborne Division. The church is about 900 meters from the Patton Memorial on the right side of the road.

Figure 10 St Peter's Church (From Author's Collection)

The area around the church is known as St Peter's square. This plot was laid out in the middle of the 19th century on the site of a former cemetery. There is a cross near the entrance to the church to remind visitors of the presence of a "field of eternal rest."

The St Peter's Church dates back to 893. The tower of the church which is 11 (33 feet) meters wide and 20 meters (60 feet) high is Norman style but the rest is Gothic.

The interior of the church has vaulted ceiling was painted in 1536 with scenes from the Old and New Testaments and effigies of patron saints. There is a Baroque pulpit designed by Luxembourg sculptor Jean-Georges Scholtus.

There is a gate located behind the church known as the Treves or Trier Gate. The gate along with the rest of the city walls was built in 1336 by order of John the Blind. He was the count of Luxembourg, king of Bohemia and Poland. The gate is 8 meters (26 feet wide) and 17 meters (56 feet high). The tower remains in its original state with the exception of the roof. The original roof was pyramid-shaped.

King Louis XIV ordered the defensive walls of Bastogne to be torn down in 1688 when the city was captured during the War of Devolution. This gate was the only portion of the wall that survived the destruction. You can still see a small portion of the old city wall on each side of the gate.

The older people of the town still refer to the gate as "the prison." The structure was used as a jail until 1877 but it was mostly used to house drunks and trouble makers, not hardened criminals.

Figure 11 Old City Gate (From Author's Collection)

There is one important item for military history enthusiasts at the church that is worth photographing. As you walk past the church with the building on your right you will come to a small red, white, and blue obelisk or Borne. This is marker number 1146 on the Liberty Road. The final marker is at the entrance to the parking lot of the Bastogne War Museum.

From the borne by the church look to the left across the street you will see the Bastogne War Memorial (8). This memorial is dedicated to the citizens of Bastogne who gave their lives during the two World Wars.

The building behind the memorial is a former seminary which now houses 2 museums. You can see the top of the steeple of the chapel that the 101st Airborne Division used as its aid station in the background over the top of the building from here.

Figure 12 Memorial in Front of I was 20 in 45 in Bastogne Expo (From Author's Collection)

Cross the street so you are on the same side of the street as the old seminary. Proceed to your left at the memorial pictured above. As you walk past with the building on your right you will see a small courtyard with a tank turret. Enter this area and go into the door on the left.

Figure 13 Figure 14 Entrance to I was 20 in 45 in Bastogne Expo (From Author's Collection)

The museum that is of interest for this tour is the "I was 20 in 45 in Bastogne Expo" (9) which can be seen right behind the memorial in the above picture. This museum is spread over 2 floors of the old seminary. There are exhibits from equipment and weapons to recreations of both American and German command posts. There are also displays that give the visitor a feeling of what it was like to be inside one of the bombed out houses.

More information about the museum can be found at: http://www.ftlb.be/en/attractions/musee/fiche.php?avi_id=832

When you finish here go back to the street and turn right following along the road with the building to your right. You will come to a roundabout with a gated parking lot as the first turn off on your right. Go into the parking lot and turn right going back in the direction from which you came. The chapel you see in the back right corner of the parking lot is the actual 101st Airborne Division aid station (10). This was the chapel for the seminary that used to be in the building that is around it.

Figure 15 101st Aid Station (From Author's Collection)

The next stop will be the 101st Airborne Division command post or NUTS! Cave (11) located at the Bastogne Barracks formally Heinz Barracks. Turn right when you leave the parking lot of the aid station. To get to the command post go down Rue le

La Roche, the second turn off from the roundabout from here.

The command post is located just down the road on your right across the street from the Bastogne cemetery. Make sure to check on tour times before you go to the museum. The last tour is conducted at 1400 as of the printing of this guide. The only way to see the museum is with a guide.

Figure 16 Entrance to Bastogne Barracks (From Author's Collection)

You can e-mail Johnny Bona, the commandant of at johnny.bona@mil.be for more information about opening times and to make a reservation for groups. They will also do special guided tours outside of scheduled times for groups. Entrance to the museum is free for individuals and for groups.

Figure 17 Gen McAuliffe's Headquarters (From Author's Collection)

The picture above is inside the office BG McAuliffe had in the basement of the building on Heinz Barracks. The location of McAuliffe's office was verified by several veterans who visited McAuliffe at this location.

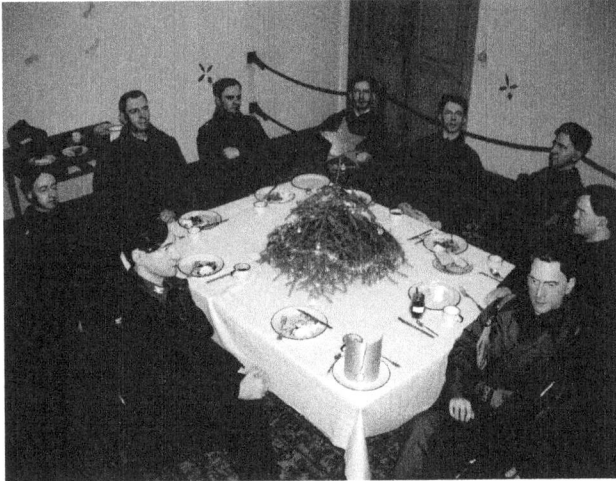

Figure 18 Christmas Dinner in NUTS!! Cave (From Author's Collection)

The picture above is a recreation of the Christmas dinner of 1944 in the NUTS! Cave. The original picture is available in the room so you can make comparisons. The people around the table from left to right are Col William L. Roberts 10th Armored Division, Lt Col Ned D. Moore 101st Airborne Division, BG Gerald J. Higgins 101st Airborne Division, BG Anthony C. McAuliffe 101st Airborne Division, Col Thomas L. Sherburne 101st Airborne Division, Lt Col Harry W. O. Kinnard 101st Airborne Division, Lt Col Carl Kohls 101st Airborne Division, Maj Paul Danahy 101st Airborne Division, and Col Curtis Renfro 101st Airborne Division.

The recreation is pretty accurate with one exception. If you look closely at the plates you will see what looks like chicken or turkey bones and other items. The actual menu for the officers was sardines and crackers.

You can visit Renee Lemaire's grave if you would like. She is buried in the cemetery that across the road from the Bastogne Barracks.

When you exit the Bastogne Barracks look across the road and you will see an entrance to the cemetery across the road just to your right. Enter the cemetery through this gate. There is a walkway to your right as soon as you enter the cemetery. Walk straight up the path from here. Turn right at the 4th path on the right counting the one just inside the entrance. You will see a tall cylindrical tree that is taller than the rest in that area. There is a path to the left just past this tree. Renee's grave is next to the tree as you turn left.

Figure 19 Renee Lemaire's Grave (From Author's Collection)

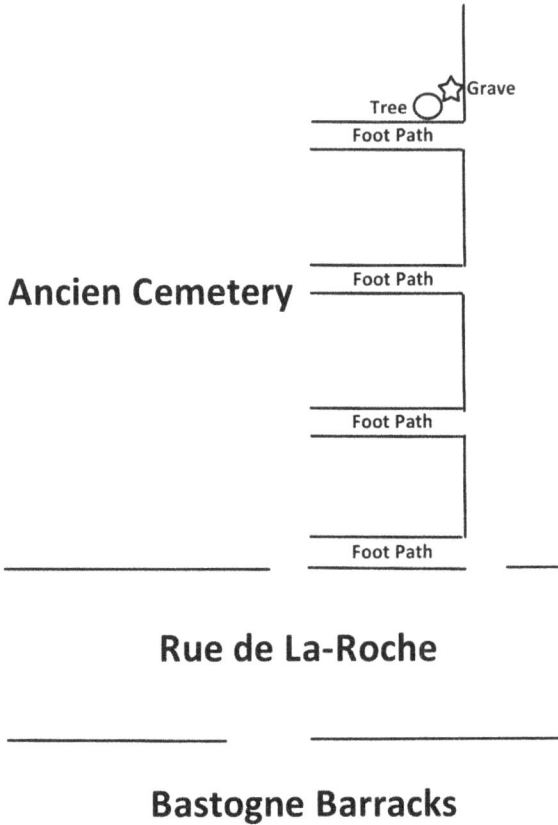

Figure 20 Map to Renee Lemaire's Grave

This is the last of the sites in the city. Now you will have to go back to your car to continue the tour.

Your tour will continue beginning at the tank turret which is a memorial to Combat Command B of the 10th Armored Division which is on the way to the Bastogne War Museum.

Robert R. Allen

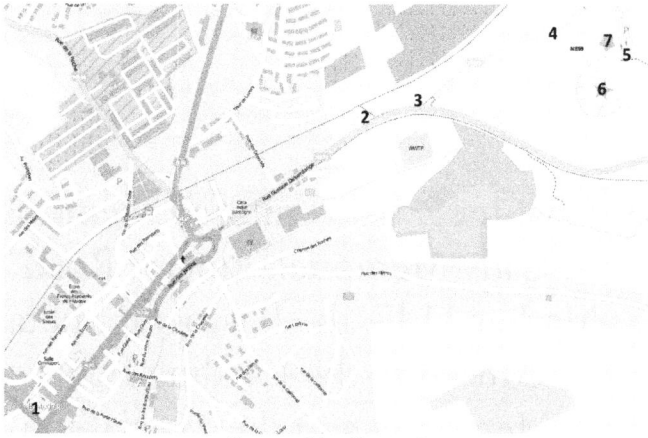

Bastogne Map Chapter 2

1. Information Center
2. 10th Armored Division Memorial
3. Cady Memorial
4. Liberty Road Marker 1147
5. Landing Eagle Memorial (101st Airborne)
6. Mardasson Memorial
7. Bastogne War Museum

Chapter 2 10th Armored Memorial, Cady Memorial, Liberty Road Marker 1147, the Bastogne Military Museum, the Landing Eagle Memorial, and the Mardasson Memorial

This portion of your visit will again start at the Information Center (1). You will need to approach the traffic light with the Information Center on your left. Turn left at the traffic light onto Rue de Vivier. Approximately 450 meters down the road you will have to turn right to follow the one way road. Continue to follow this route, Rue des Jardins, until you get to the roundabout. You will pass Saint Peter's Church and Trier Gate on the left. Take the first exit off the roundabout.

Approximately 550 meters down the road you will see a tank turret on the left side of the road. This memorial dedicated to Combat Command B of the 10th Armored Division. The memorial was dedicated on December 10, 2011 (2). The turret is from a

Sherman tank that was assigned to the 10th Armored Division.

Figure 21 10th Armored Division Memorial (From Author's Collection)

The plaque at the base of the turret reads:

The U.S. 10TH Armored Division' Combat Command B, the first major combat unit to defend Bastogne, arrived on the evening of December 18, 1944. Colonel William L. Roberts deployed his Combat Command in three teams:

Team Desobry at Noville
Team Cherry at Neffe and Longvilly
Team O'Hara at Wardin and Marvie

After delaying the Garman advance, the remnants of these 10th Armored teams joined the U.S.

101st Airborne Division for the remainder of the siege. In recognition of their gallant actions, Combat Command B was awarded the Presidential Unit Citation.

Dedicated by the 10th Armored Division Veterans December 10, 2011

It's important to remember the role this unit played in the defense of Bastogne. These the men arrived in Bastogne on December 18, 1944 and were rushed to the east and southeast to hold off the Germans until the 101st Airborne Division could arrive.

Now go back to the road and turn left. Drive for approximately 150 meters and turn left at the Cady Memorial (3) that is on the corner of Rue de Clervaux. This is a memorial dedicated to Corporal Emile Cady Premier Chasseur Ardennais or the Premier Light Infantry Ardennes. This unit was based near Bastogne. Cpl Cady is recorded as the first Belgian to die in the defense of Bastogne. The plaque on the memorial reads:

STOP IF YOU ARE PASSING
Here on the 10th May 1940 died the hero
Corporal Cady
First Ardennes Chasseurs
Fell for the defense of Bastogne

The boar's head on the left of the memorial is the insignia of Cpl Cady's unit. He was killed during the initial blitzkrieg when Belgium fell to the Germans.

Figure 22 Cady Memorial (From Author's Collection)

The entrance to the Bastogne War Museum and the Mardasson Memorial is approximately 400 meters up the road on the right. The final marker, Km 1147 of the Liberty Road (4) is located on the left side of the drive as you enter the parking area.

The Liberty Road is a commemorative route marking the advance of the allied armies through France. The route covers mainly the path of General Bradley's 1st Army Group and General Patton's 3rd Army. The 0 Km "Borne" marker is located in St Mere Eglise the first town liberated by the Americans on D-Day. The actual first marker on the physical route, borne 00, is at Utah Beach signifying the start of the route. This marker has the emblem of the American 1st Army Group at the base.

Figure 23 Liberty Road Marker 1147 (From Author's Collection)

There are two paths to the memorial route. One goes to Metz which follows a large portion of Patton's advance. The other ends in Bastogne.

The first actual road sign marking the Liberty Road is in St Marie du Mont, which happens to be a major objective of the 101st Airborne Division on D-Day.

The Liberty Road was the idea of Guy de la Vasselais as a memorial to the liberation of France, Voie de la Liberte`. Several routes were considered with the one Patton took to Metz was considered to be the most "glorious." The Liberty Road was finally officially opened on September 18, 1947 with a ceremony at Fontainebleau, France which was liberated on August 23, 1944.

Figure 24 The Landing Eagle Memorial (From Author's Collection)

When you reach the parking lot and walk toward the museum that will be on your right you will see the Landing Eagle Memorial (5) on your left. This memorial was dedicated to the 101st Airborne by the city of Bastogne.

The plaque on the front reads:

"May this eagle always symbolize the sacrifices and heroism of the 101st Airborne Division and all its attached units."

December 1944 – January 1945
The City and Citizens of Bastogne

The plaque that is on the right side as you face the memorial gives thanks and recognizes the other units that fought at Bastogne. The rest of the units may have been forgotten in history because each group was made up of a relatively small number of men. It is also possible people get confused because all units in Bastogne fell under the command of the 101st Airborne Division.

It's important to remember that other units also played a role in the valiant defense of Bastogne. In his book "Beyond the Band of Brothers" Dick Winters points out that it was obvious that a "terrific battle" had taken place in the Bois Jacques before the 101st Airborne Division arrived. Bill Guarnere mentioned in his book "Brothers in Battle Best of Friends" that everyone in the 101st Airborne Division was glad that the 10th Armored Division was there before they arrived.

So to give credit where credit is due, the following is a list of the other units that fought so bravely in Bastogne. Keep in mind that there may have been small groups of men from other units that weren't identified.

- Combat Command B 10th Armored Division

- Combat Command Regimental 9th Armored Division
- 705th Tank Destroyer Battalion
- 35th Combat Engineer Battalion
- 158th Combat Engineer Battalion
- 58th Armored Field Artillery Battalion
- 420th Armored Filed Artillery Battalion
- 755th Field Artillery Battalion of 8th Corps
- 969th Field Artillery Battalion of 8th Corps
- Team SNAFU

The men of these units made up about one half of the force that defended Bastogne. Many of the units had already taken a beating from the Germans as they pushed into Belgium.

Continue on with this memorial to your left to get to the Mardasson Memorial.

Figure 25 Mardasson Memorial (From Author's Collection)

The Mardasson Memorial (6) is dedicated to the 76,890 Americans who were wounded or killed during the Battle of the Bulge not just at Bastogne.

The Mardasson Memorial is located where a memorial was to be built in memory of President Harry S. Truman. This was not to be. On July 4, 1946 it was decided that a memorial commemorating the sacrifices made by the men who defended Bastogne and the area of the bulge would be built on the site instead. The idea evolved into what you see now.

The star shaped structure is 12 meters (36 feet) high and has a side width of 31 meters (93 feet). The open area in the center of the structure is 20 meters (60 feet). The monument was finally completed and dedicated on July 16, 1950.

The inner walls have paintings which depicting scenes from the battle. The names of all 48 states that were in the union during WWII are engraved around the top of the memorial. There are also engravings of the units that fought in the battle on the pillars that support the structure.

As you face the memorial look to the right and you will see signs that lead to the crypt. There are three alters dedicated to the Protestant, Catholic, and Jewish faiths in the crypt. The Protestant alter is directly across from the entrance with the Jewish alter on the left and the Catholic alter on the right.

The crypt was carved and decorated by a French artist named Fernand Leger. The inscription on the memorial stone reads:

LIBERATORIBVS
AMERICANIS
POPVLVS BELGICVS
MEMOR
IV.VII.MCMXLVI

The inscription translates into: "The Belgian people remember their American liberators 4 July 1946".

The crypt is now secured behind a gate to prevent vandalism.

Figure 26 View inside the Crypt (From Author's Collection)

As you return to the parking lot you will see the Bastogne War Museum (7). The museum is currently being renovated with a scheduled opening date of the summer 2014. The current museum is being incorporated into the new facility. You can get more information about the museum at: http://www.bastognewarmuseum.be/uk-bastogne-war-museum.html.

Figure 27 Bastogne Historical Center (From Author's Collection)

The current museum has its roots in the efforts of one man; Guy Franz Arend. The evolution of the museum took 63 years and a lot of effort.

In the beginning the museum was simply called the Bastogne NUTS Museum which opened in 1950. Arend had many supporters including one that would not seem so obvious, General of the Panzer Armee Hasso von Manteuffel, the general who was a main contributor to the "Wacht am Rhein" offensive we know as the Battle of the Bulge. He was also in command of the 5th SS Panzer Armee tasked with capturing Bastogne.

The museum was moved to Maison Siville but was moved again when the building was demolished in 1954. This is when it was moved to Place du Carre on Place McAuliffe.

The items on exhibit were first collected from the battlefield before locals could scavenge them in an attempt to rebuild their lives. Later the museum received many donations from veterans and collectors to help make the displays more complete.

It wasn't until 1965 that Mr Arend received permission to move the museum to its current location. The land belonged to the Bastogne tourist office and they were not an easy group to deal with. It took 10 years of negotiations before Arend was allowed to build the museum. Many believe the delay was because Mr Arend wanted the building to be star shaped.

The old Bastogne Historical Center, which is the heart of the current museum, was first opened on May 31, 1976. There was a big celebration for the museum's opening combined with the bi-centennial celebrations of American independence.

The Bastogne tourist office bought Mr Arend's collection in 2000 and began raising funds to renovate the building. In 2004 the tourist office received money from the Ministry of Tourism which not only funded the renovations but also paid for the audio guides available for your visit.

The current renovation has not been without its own challenges. The camps were divided on the purpose of the museum once it's reopened. One group wanted it to remain as a museum dedicated to the Battle of the Bulge while another wanted it to be a World War II museum. The second group won. The museum will reopen as the Bastogne War Museum.

The vehicle that is usually in front of the museum is not a tank. This is actually an M-10 tank destroyer. These vehicles are usually lighter and faster than a tank and the turret is open.

The M-10 is built on the chassis of the M4 Sherman Tank. It weighs 30 tons with a top speed of about 50 miles an hour. The crews depended on the speed and maneuverability to keep them out of the way of the German tanks because the M-10, like most tank destroyers, is very lightly armored.

Although the M-10 could outrun its opponents the main job of this tank killer is obvious by its name. The M-10 was also lightly armed, especially if it had to face a King Tiger or Panther, that it didn't stand a chance. Its 3" 76 mm gun was no match for the thick armor of these tanks.

Robert R. Allen

Bastogne Map Chapter 3

1. The Bois de la Paix (Wood of Peace)
2. Easy Company Memorial
3. Bois Jacques/Easy Company Foxholes
4. Shifty Powers Sniper House

Chapter 3 The Bois de le Paix, The Bois Jacques, and Foy

The next portion of this book will take you to the some of the locations where Easy Company fought and point out a very interesting memorial to all those who fought in Bastogne, the Bois de la Paix (Wood of Peace).

To continue your journey turn right as you exit the parking lot of the Bastogne War Museum onto Chemin de Marvie/Route de Bizory. Follow the road for approximately 2 km and turn left toward Foy. Approximately 400 meters up the road you will see a sign on the right for Bois de la Paix (Wood of Peace). This is a wooded area planted by UNICEF in remembrance of the individuals who fought at Bastogne

The Bois de la Paix (Wood of Peace) (1) is a collection of approximately 4000, mostly birch, beech, and oak, trees planted by UNICEF. The trees form the shape of the organizations logo, the face of a mother looking down at her child, a symbol of human tenderness. There are posts in the ground by each tree where plaques with the names of Bastogne veterans can be placed.

The site was officially opened in 1994 for the 50th anniversary of the siege of Bastogne. Each of the veterans who returned for the opening ceremony had his name placed on a plaque. The site is dedicated to all the Americans, Belgians, and civilians who died during December – January 1944 – 1945.

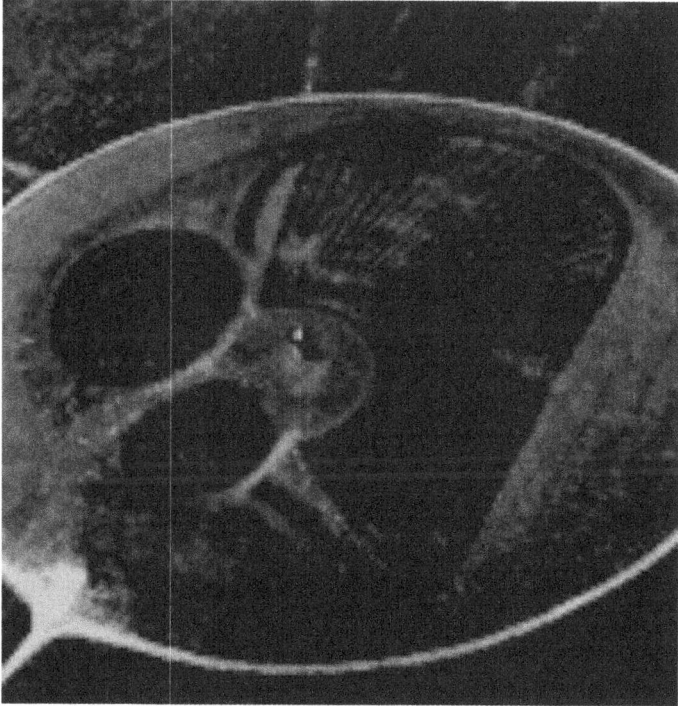

Figure 28 Bois de la Paix (Peace Woods)

Continue down the road another 800 meters to the Easy Company Memorial (2). The memorial is located across the road from where the old train station was located which is now a private home. The area to the left of the old railroad track as you face the memorial was the responsibility of the 501st PIR and the wooded area on the right, the Bois Jacques (the Jack Woods) was the responsibility of Easy Company and the rest of the 506th PIR.

Figure 29 Easy Company Memorial (From Author's Collection)

The Easy Company Memorial located in the area where the company was first deployed. The company also spent time here at other times during the battle. The memorial was dedicated on June 10, 2005. The dedication was attended by some of the surviving members of the company. The panel on the left side of memorial lists the names of the 14 men who died in the defense of Bastogne and push to Noville and Rachamps. The panel on the right side reads:

In the wood behind this monument, on 18 December 1944 "E" Company of the 506th P.I.R 101ST Airborne division U.S. Army dug their foxholes in the Bois Jacques Woods as part of the defence (sic) perimeter of Bastogne City that was soon to be surrounded by several enemy divisions. The circumstances were dreadful with constant mortar, rocket and artillery fire, snow fall, temperatures below -28 Celsius at night with little food and ammunition. The field hospital had been captured so little medical help was available. On December 24th the "E" company position was attacked at dawn by about 45 enemy soldiers. The attack failed and "E" Company held their position with 1 casualty against 23 of the enemy. The position of "E" Company was twice bombed and strafed by American P 47's. During the periods of January 9th and January 13th "E" Company suffered its most casualties ending with the attack and capture of Foy on January 13th. 8 were killed in Foy and 6 earlier. During the whole period 32 were wounded and another 21 were evacuated with cold weather illnesses. In many units involved in the defence (sic) of Bastogne the casualties were even greater. This monument is dedicated to all that fought and symbolic of what happened to other units during the Battle of the Bulge.

Airborne Always, Men of E Company

This memorial is the source a lot of bad feelings because it seems like the men of Easy Company are getting all the recognition while others are being ignored. This seems a little odd because the inscription on the memorial says it is dedicated to all the units that fought to defend Bastogne.

The Bastogne – Gouvy railroad ran though the area during the war. The tracks acted as a kind of dividing line between the 501st PIR and 506th PIR during the battle.

The following map shows the position of the 101st Airborne Division units as well as the German attacks during December 19-23, 1944.

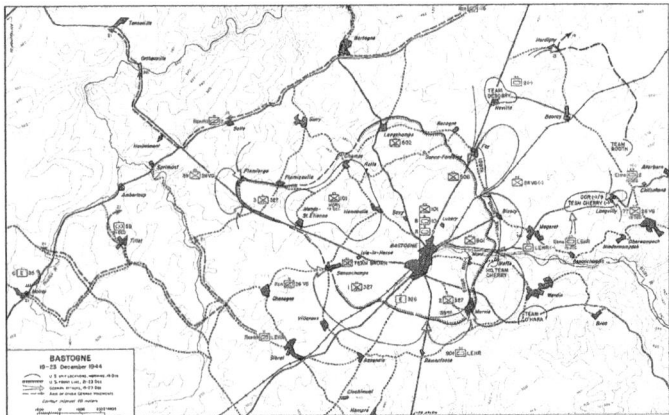

Bastogne Situation Map 19 – 23 December 1944

If you look closely you'll notice that most of the German attacks were conducted by the 26th Volksgrenadier. This is because von Manteuffel originally planned to go around Bastogne and leave the infantry to capture the city.

Gen von Manteuffel was forced to change his tactics once he realized that it was the 101st Airborne Division that was sent to hold the city. This forced von Manteuffel to leave a portion of the Panzer Lehr to assist in the capture of the city. This weakened the force pushing to the Meuse River.

Now proceed up the road another 600 meters. You will see a dirt area on the left side of the road with a logging path on the left as you face the open area (3).

Figure 30 Entrance to Foxholes (From Author's Collection)

Follow this logging trail for approximately 100 meters and you will see a path that leads off to the right. Take this trail into the woods.

Figure 31 Trail into Foxholes (From Author's Collection)

You will find several foxholes from Easy Company in this area of the woods. You will also find foxholes at the end of the trail where it comes to the clearing that leads down to Foy.

The area to the right and left of this trail is where you will find some of the best preserved of the original foxholes of Easy Company. Don't be fooled by the holes that are the result of trees being blown out of the ground. There are enough foxholes to give you an opportunity to get several pictures of the good ones.

Follow the path until you reach the place where you can see an opening in the trees. There will be a row of trees that continue to the right and left with the opening facing toward the town of Foy. This is the area that Babe Heffron and Bill Guarnere identified as the place where their foxholes were located.

Figure 32 View to Foy (From Author's Collection)

Go to your right while facing Foy and walk back toward the road. You will find several very well preserved foxholes in this area. These foxholes were there because there were Germans dug in on the other side of the road.

It is necessary to warn you that there are a lot of rotted tree stumps here that make wonderful nests for wasps so be careful. You will notice that the foxholes aren't exactly the 6X6X6 versions required by Capt Sobel but they served their purpose. You will also notice that many are dug next to the trees to take advantage of the extra protection from both the tree and its root structure.

Figure 33 Easy Company Foxhole (From Author's Collection)

Although Easy Company spent much of the time in this area this not where the company was located during the attack on Foy 13 Dec 1944. The company was on the other side of the Foy Bastogne road and attacked from the direction of Recogne. It was the only company from 2nd Battalion that participated in the initial attack. The rest of the attacking force was made up of the men from 3rd Battalion Item Company, which attacked advancing up the Bastogne-Foy road headed toward Noville.

It was during this attack that Lt Norman Dike completely broke down. He froze and stopped the entire company in the middle of an open field leaving the exposed to enemy gun fire.

This is when Capt Winters took action and made a decision that would change the war for Easy. Knowing he could not take command himself, although he truly wanted to, he looked for someone else. He turned and there was Lt Ronald Speirs. Winters sent Speirs to relieve Dike which probably saved the lives of many of the men and ensured the attack would be a success.

After Foy was finally secured Col Sink asked Capt Winters what he was going to do about Easy Company's command issue. Winters was confused because the decision should have been made by Lt Col Strayer the battalion commander. Winters simply replied that he was relieving Dike and putting Speirs in command of Easy Company. Sink agreed and Lt Ronald Speirs would command Easy Company through the rest of the war.

Now you will leave the foxholes and continue down the road toward Foy.

Approximately 1 Km down the road you will come to a left turn in the road with a road sign that directs you toward Foy. You will see the traffic light on the Bastogne-Foy road when you make the turn.

Approximately 85 meters after you turn you will see a house on the left that runs long ways to the road. This is the house (4) where Shifty Powers killed the German sniper as depicted in the mini-series. The sniper was in the upstairs window of the house.

1st Sgt Lipton and Pvt Popeye Winn went into the house after Shifty killed the sniper. When they got upstairs to where the sniper was they saw that the man had been shot in the middle of the forehead. Popeye looked at Lipton and simply said, "You know it just doesn't pay to be shootin' at Shifty when he's got a rife."

Figure 34 Shift Powers Sniper House (From Author's Collection)

When you stand looking at the house from the angle show in the picture above you can see several pock marks from bullets. There is also evidence of the battle on the buildings around this house.

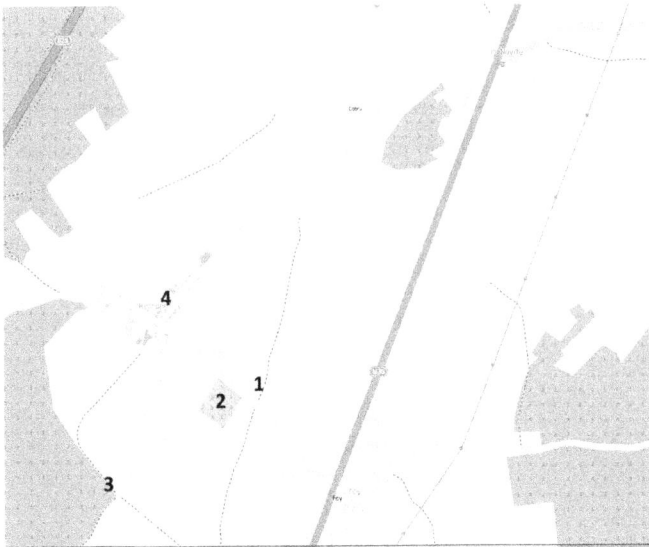

Bastogne Map Chapter 4

1. Temporary Cemetery
2. German Cemetery
3. American Indian Memorial
4. Recogne Aid Station Church

Chapter 4 Temporary Cemetery, German Cemetery, American Indian Memorial, 2nd Battalion, Noville, and Rachamps

Continue through the intersection toward Recogne. Approximately 600 meters up the road you will come to an intersection. Turn right at this intersection. You will come to a memorial on your left that marks the location of the temporary cemetery (1) used during the Battle of Bastogne.

Many of the remains that were not sent back to the states after the war were moved to one of the American cemeteries. They are spread out between the cemetery in Hamm, Luxembourg, Margraten, Holland, and Henri Chapelle, Belgium. There are 5 members of Easy Company laid to rest in Luxembourg. The men here are Warren (Skip) Muck E-9-45, Kenneth Webb G-4-20, Patrick Neil B-9-34, John Julian F-10-24, and Alex Penkala I-9-5.

Figure 35 Memorial at Temporary Cemetery (From Author's Collection)

The engraving under the American and Belgian flag reads: "Here lies the site of the FOY AMERICAN TEMPORARY CEMETERY From 1945 to 1948 It served as a temporary resting field for 2,701 Americans killed in action during THE BATTLE OF THE BULGE 12 -16 – 1944 * 1 -28 – 1945

The poem in the lower center portion of the memorial reads:

We have only died in vain if you believe so;
You have to decide the wisdom of our choice,
By the world which you shall build upon our
headstones,
And the everlasting truth, in which have your voice.

Though dead, we are not heroes yet, nor can be,
'Til the living by their lives which are the tools,
Carve us the epitaph of wise men,
And give us not the epitaph of fools.

David F. Phillips, 506th PIR 101st Airborne

Now go back to the intersection and turn right to continue on toward Recogne.

Approximately 200 meters up the road on you left you come to the German cemetery (2). This is where many of the German soldiers were buried. Unlike the Americans, the Germans do not return their war dead to Germany so you will find many small cemeteries located around Europe. The German cemeteries also continue to expand in many cases. It is estimated that Germany is still finding approximately 40,000 war casualties per year and they don't even search the sites with fewer than 50 graves.

Figure 36 Recogne German Cemetery (From Author's Collection)

After the war the Belgians began collecting the German war dead from small field cemeteries and placing them into centralized locations. In 1954 the Germans reached an agreement with the Belgians to gain the right to maintain the German cemeteries. The cemetery at Recogne is one of the largest of these sites from the battle with a total of 6,809 remains. Once in control of the cemetery, the Germans were able to identify 1,121 of the remains.

In 1956 an international group from 6 countries placed a wall around the cemetery. The group had the motto "Taking care of the graves." The crosses are gray sandstone and each has the names of 6 dead, three on each side.

Continue up the road another 350 meters and turn left. Now drive for approximately 850 until you reach the tree line. It will be easier to get to the next memorial if you leave your car here. Follow the path to your right for approximately 50-60 meters. Here you will find the memorial dedicated to the American Indians (3) who died in the struggle to liberate Belgium. This is also the area where 2nd Battalion launched its attack on Noville.

Figure 37 American Indian Memorial (From Author's Collection)

The inscription on the plaque reads:

"In the Loving Memory of the American Indian Soldiers Fallen for the Liberation of Belgium."

This is the area where 3rd Battalion was during the majority of the battle. The 3rd Battalion was made up of G,H, and I companies. The 2nd Battalion was in an area on the right flank of 3rd Battalion on the night when Skip Muck and Alex Penkala were killed.

Follow the road back to the intersection where you came from and turn left when you get there.

Continue down the road for about 80 meters and turn right onto the road toward Cobru. Just down the road on the left you will see a church that was used as an aid station during the battle (4). They usually have a re-enactment camp set up in Recogne during the yearly Bastogne Memorial Walk. The church here is open and displayed as it would have looked during the battle.

Figure 38 Recogne Church/Aid Station (From Author's Collection)

Continue on this road through Cobru all the way to Noville. As you proceed look to your left and you will see a ridge that runs parallel to the road a little ways in the distant. This is Vaux Ridge. This is where Capt Winters led 2nd Battalion during its attack on Noville.

If you turn right at this intersection and drive to the memorial marker on the left side of the road you will find a memorial to some of the men of Noville who were murdered by the Germans. At the memorial marker stand with your back to the road and the memorial marker on your right. Walk away from the road and you will see the memorial cemetery dedicated to Abbe Delvaux Louis and 7 others who were executed by the Germans on the left. The men were accused of aiding the Americans during the battle to delay the Germans from reaching Bastogne. These men were singled out from an original group of 60 from the town.

Figure 39 Noville Memorial (From Author's Collection)

To continue following the route of Easy Company through the end of their time fighting in

Belgium turn around here and head away from Bastogne. If you did not go to the memorial mentioned above turn left when you get to the intersection in Noville. Now drive for approximately 2 Km the turn right toward Rachamps. Follow the road into Rachamps until you see the church in front of you just to the right.

The company spent its last night in the Ardennes in the church in Rachamps. The sisters called in the girl's choir to entertain the men while they relaxed. They all thought they would be returning to France to recover and take on replacements the following day. This would have to wait since the next stop for Easy Company and the 101st Airborne Division was Haguenau, France.

Figure 40 Rachamps Church (From Author's Collection)

In Rachamps you will find a plaque dedicated to the 101st Airborne marking the location of the Tree of Freedom that is outside the church where the company spent its last night in the Ardennes. When you come to the intersection where the church is in front of you just the right you see blue road signs across the intersection. The plaque is a short distance behind the road signs.

Figure 41 Plaque Dedicated to 101st Airborne in Rachamps (From Author's Collection)

The inscription on the plaque reads:

Tree of Freedom planted on September 21st, 2002 by the children of the village and the American veterans of E Company, 506th Regiment, 101st Airborne

(Band of Brothers) present in Rachamps during offensive 1944-45.

Now return to the traffic light in the center of Bastogne to continue your tour. At the light continue driving straight to reach the Glessener Memorial.

Bastogne Map Chapter 5

1. Glessener Memorial
2. Pillbox

Chapter 5 Glessener Memorial and Pillbox

There is a memorial on the way out of town dedicated to Cpl Ernest Glessener (1). It is located on Rue de Neufchateau about 1 Km from the traffic light by McAuliffe Square. To get there if you start at the Information Center go to the light with the Information Center on your left and turn right at the light, continue down the road until you see the memorial on your right.

Figure 42 Glessener Memorial (From Author's Collection)

The text on the memorial reads: This monument has been erected by the grateful town of Bastogne to the memory of Ernest Glessener the first G.I. killed on this spot on September 10, 1944 after having destroyed a German tank. This occurred during the first liberation of Bastogne which occurred on September 16, 1944.

Although this is a nice sentiment there is one problem, according to the records of the units that fought in Bastogne there was never a Cpl Glessener who served in the area of Bastogne during this time period.

The last location to be cover may be the most important to the outcome of the siege because the actions here allowed re-enforcements to arrive along with much needed supplies as well as opening a corridor to enable the evacuation of the wounded. This is the pillbox (2) located to the southwest of Bastogne where the spearhead of the 4th Armored Division of Patton's 3rd Army broke the siege on December 26, 1944.

Figure 43 Pillbox Where 4th Armored Division Broke Siege (From Author's Collection)

To get to the pillbox continue down Rue de Neufchateau from the Glessener memorial for approximately 1 Km then turn left. Follow the sign toward Assenois but make sure to watch carefully for the sign. It is very close to the ground and easy to miss.

After you turn drive for about 550 meters to the intersection and turn left. The pillbox will be just down the road on the right.

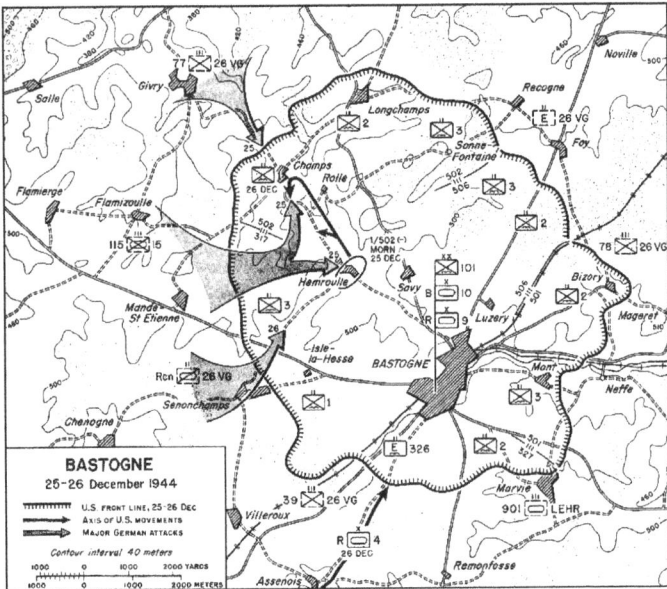

Bastogne Situation Map 25-25 December 1944

The map above shows the action around Bastogne during the 25 – 26 December 1944. Notice the attack on the northwest side of the town. This was one of the strongest, concentrated attacks made during the siege. The attacks of December 25-26, 1944 took place in the area that was defended by the 502nd PIR and the 463rd Parachute Field Artillery Battalion.

The arrow annotated at the bottom center of the map to the right of the legend from Assenois is the route taken by the 4th Armored Division during its approach to Bastogne.

Figure 44 Cobra King First Tank into Bastogne

The Cobra King, pictured above, commanded by 1st Lt Charles Boggess was the first tank to break the siege at Bastogne. Lt Boggess and his crew of Cpl Milton Dickerman and Pvts James G. Murphy, Hubert S. Smith, and Harold Hafner broke through at 1650 on December 26, 1944 and linked up with the Able Company of 326th Airborne Engineering Battalion of the 101st Airborne Division.

The 4th Armored Division approached from Assenois which is southwest of Bastogne. The unit encountered heavy resistance along the way and the resistance increased as it neared Bastogne.

The final dash into Bastogne was almost like a scene from a cowboy movie. It was getting late and would be dark soon so Lt Boggess decided he needed to make a final push to get into Bastogne. He got three tanks together and headed toward the town with the guns and turrets rotating and firing to clear a path. Lt Boggess and the Cobra King ended up far ahead of the rest of the group as the tanks approached Bastogne. The tank was verified by the serial number on the front that can be seen in the picture on the previous page.

When Lt Boggess got to the pillbox at the outside of town he saw several figures. There were reports of Germans in the area dressed as Americans so he called out but nobody answered so he called out again, "Come out here, come on out. This is the Forth Armored." Finally a single man approached the tank and said, "I'm Lt Webster of the 326th Engineers, 101st Airborne Division, Glad to see you." This meeting took place at 1650.

When Bastogne was finally turned back over to Maj Gen Troy Middleton, VIII Corps commander, the members of the 101st Airborne Division decided they wanted a memento of their stay. To this end, they had the general sign a receipt for the city of Bastogne. It's said he did this willingly and with a smile on his face. A copy of the receipt is on the following page.

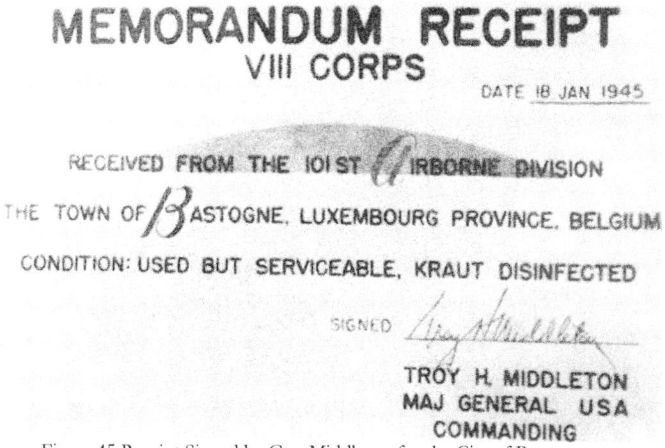

MEMORANDUM RECEIPT
VIII CORPS
DATE 18 JAN 1945

RECEIVED FROM THE 101 ST AIRBORNE DIVISION

THE TOWN OF BASTOGNE, LUXEMBOURG PROVINCE, BELGIUM

CONDITION: USED BUT SERVICEABLE, KRAUT DISINFECTED

SIGNED

TROY H. MIDDLETON
MAJ GENERAL USA
COMMANDING

Figure 45 Receipt Signed by Gen Middleton for the City of Bastogne

With the siege finally broken the road was clear to bring in much needed supplies and take out the wounded. The men of the 101st Airborne Division thought they would be returned to Mourmelon for replacements and a little R&R. Instead they were to take Foy, Recogne, Cobru, Noville, and Rachamps. Even then they weren't to get off the line. Their next stop was Haguenau, France. It wasn't till after that they were pulled off the line for much needed rest.

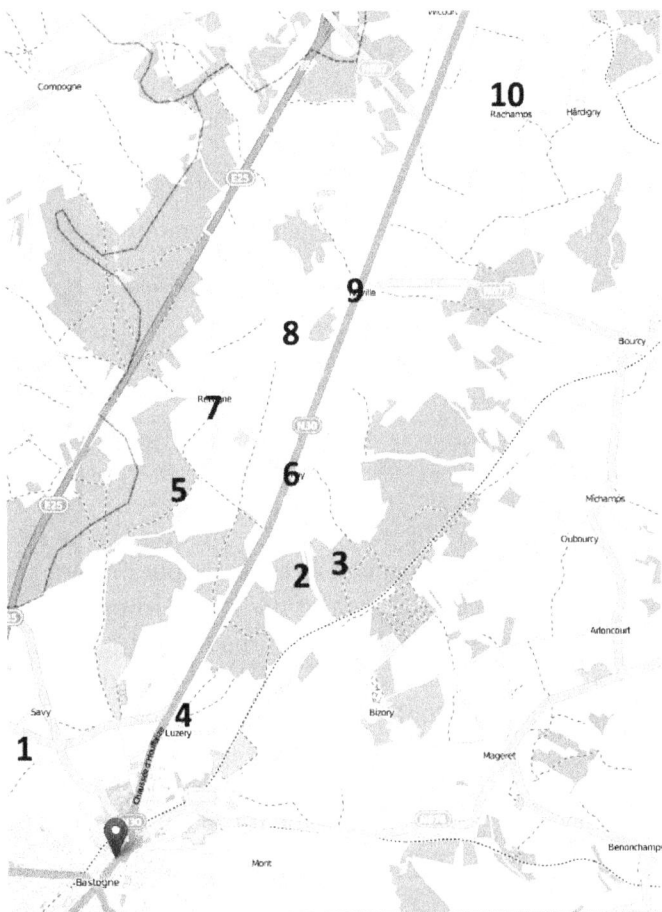

Bastogne Map Chapter 6

1. Jump off area
2. Bois Jacques
3. Bois des Corbeaux
4. Luzery
5. Fazone Woods
6. Foy
7. Recogne

8. Cobru
9. Noville
10. Rachamps

Chapter 6 Easy Company Facts: Battle for Bastogne

Easy Company arrived in the Bastogne area in 318 open top trucks southwest of Champs in an area just northwest of Bastogne on December 19, 1944 (1). They were then deployed on foot to the MLR (main line of resistance) in the Bois Jacques about 3 miles to the east.

On the way to the Bois Jacques they came across the men who were withdrawing from the battle. Some of them were running others were shuffling back with dazed looks or looks of complete fear on their faces. Some were almost screaming "they're gonna kill us all". Many of the men withdrawing were amazed that the unit was actually moving forward to face the Germans. The men of the 101st Airborne Division started scrounging all the gear they could from those who were withdrawing.

The unit reached the Bois Jacques (2) in the area near the current Easy Company Memorial on the evening of December 19, 1944 and the on December 21, 1944 Bastogne was completely surrounded. Some say that the Germans learned the hard way that the

101st Airborne Division was the wrong unit to surround. Easy Company didn't see its first real combat until December 24, 1944.

It seemed men like Gen Eisenhower realized the effect of having the 101st Airborne Division in Bastogne would be and tried to hide the fact that this was the unit that was heading to Bastogne. The men were actually ordered to remove the Screaming Eagle emblem from their shoulder. But even this didn't stop the Germans from finding out what unit was in the town.

General Eisenhower was right to assume that if the Germans knew what unit was in Bastogne would make a difference it their strategy. Gen Lüttwitz, commander of the XLVII Corps responsible to proceed through the center of the 5th Panzer Armee advance, planned on going around Bastogne at first to enable his forces to reach the Meuse River more quickly. His plan was to move his armor and artillery quickly around the city. As soon as he discovered it was the 101st Airborne Division that was in Bastogne he elected to leave a portion of the Panzer Lehr there to assist the 26th Volksgrenadier in capturing the city.

It could be argued that the role played by the 101st Airborne Division went beyond the defense of Bastogne. The strength of the force advancing toward the Meuse River was weakened because Gen Lüttwitz could not leave Bastogne in his rear with such a formidable force occupying the city.

The determination of the Easy Company and the rest of the 101st Airborne Division and their fighting skills along with the orders to hold Bastogne at all costs meant they would never give up the city. They had also heard about the murder of the 84 POWs near Malmedy meaning the Germans were not taking prisoners. This only helped to strengthen their determination to hold off the German advance.

The unit arrived in Bastogne lacking the basic essentials needed. Although most of the men had a wool overcoat there were still some who only had the thin M-42 jump jacket or M-42 field jacket, neither of which provide much warmth and are almost useless against the cold the men encountered in Bastogne. The men who had their passes cancelled and were called back from leaves went to the front in their dress uniforms.

The Corcoran jump boots they wore were no protection against the cold. They were also impossible to keep dry. Some of the men wrapped their boots in burlap and soaked them in water to freeze. They felt this approach kept their feet warmer.

Many of the weapons they previously had were supposed to be turned in after Operation Market Garden for maintenance along with the ammunition. Even though they were supposed to turn in their weapons and ammunition many of the men refused to do this which worked out to their advantage. If they had followed orders they would not have had enough weapons and the Battle of the Bulge may have ended much differently.

They received some extra ammunition once they arrived in Bastogne but it just wasn't enough. Some of the men scrounged what they could from the men who were retreating. The look on the faces of the men retreating shocked those going to the front.

Easy Company along with the rest of the 2nd Battalion replaced 1rd Battalion, which had been fighting with Team Desobry, from the 10th Armored Division, in Noville, on the line on December 20, 1944. The 10th Armored Division arrived before the 101st Airborne Division and was only there under protest from Lt Gen Patton.

Lt Gen Bradley called Patton to request the 10th Armored Division be released to assist in Bastogne but Patton refused. Then Bradley told Patton he was taking the unit. Patton was engaged in a push to cross the Rhein River and said he could not afford to lose the unit.

The men of the 101st Airborne Division were aware that the 10th Armored Division arrived before them and was leading in the defense of Bastogne. There was evidence of the battle all over.

Bill Guarnere commented that he himself, as well as the rest of the men of the 101st Airborne Division, was thankful and lucky that the 10th Armored Division was in Bastogne to hold the location until the airborne arrived.

Dick Winters said that there was evidence of a "terrible battle" in the Bois Jacques before Easy Company arrived. There were dead bodies and parts of bodies all over the forest.

The 101st Airborne Division deployed the morning after arriving to ensure the city of Bastogne was effectively defended. The 506th Parachute Infantry Regiment was deployed to the Bois Jacques east of the city. The 502nd PIR circling around to the north of Bastogne, was on the left flank of the 506th PIR and the 501st PIR circling round to the south of Bastogne was on the right flank of the 506th PIR. The 327th Glider Infantry Regiment, along with the 326th Airborne Engineer Battalion, was positioned between the 501st PIR and 502nd PIR to the west and southwest of the city.

Even though the men of the 101st Airborne Division would occupy the area around Bastogne for almost a month Earl McClung said he never saw the city. He spent the entire time in the Bois Jacques.

The 506th PIR occupied the Bois Jacques on the left side of a road that runs between Bizory and Foy. The 501st PRI was on their right flank with the Germans right across the road. The 3rd battalion of the 506th PIR was directly on Easy Company's left flank and Easy, Fox, and Dog companies occupied the center and right flank of the line during the battle.

Capt Winters set up the 2nd Battalion command post far enough behind the line to prevent harassment from small arms fire but close enough to keep contact with the flow of the battle. He also placed the command post behind 2nd Battalion so it shaded toward Easy Company's usual position.

There was one point during the battle when Germans were able to take advantage of a gap in the line near the location of the current Easy Company Memorial to set up a defensive position. The Germans were able to dig in and put up a strong fight before the 101st Airborne Division was able to push them back out for good.

Easy Company set up a line of defense not only toward the city of Foy but also along the Bizory/Foy road. The company also had to keep an eye on the Germans that were just across the road. When you walk along the tree line next to the road you will find many very well preserved foxholes.

Easy Company was tasked to clear the Bois Jacques along with the rest of the 506th PIR. Once this was accomplished the men dug foxholes and set up defensive positions.

The first night proved to be very confusing for the men setting up defenses because there were no clear boundaries between the individual units. Incidents like the one depicted in the mini-series of the German soldier wandering through the line actually happened quite often. Easy Company's right flank, where the 501st PIR was supposed to be, was often exposed during the battle.

Capt Winters credits Captain Nixon's liaison work between 2nd Battalion and regiment as being a major reason for the success of the unit. Although Capt Nixon was assigned to the regiment at the time of the battle he spent most of his time on the line with 2nd Battalion and Capt Winters.

Capt Nixon's drinking habits are very well documented. Capt Winters made no attempts to change the habits of his friend. It seemed like a very odd relationship since Capt Winters was a strict non-drinker. As it turned out Nixon's nocturnal nature from his drinking habits was actually an advantage. Being a morning person Capt Winters kept an eye on things during the day and Capt Nixon took over at night.

The company encountered its first taste of heavy shelling on December 23-24, 1944. The men were desperate for anything to provide extra cover over their foxholes to protect them from flying shrapnel and pieces of trees. While some would use tree branches, others used dead German soldiers. Although the bombardment was bad, other 101st Airborne Division units around Bastogne had faced worse up to that point and for Easy Company the worst was yet to come.

Easy Company spent Christmas Eve on the line listening to the city of Bastogne being bombed. This is also when they received the famous Christmas Memo from BG McAuliffe:

Headquarters 101st Airborne Division

Office of the Division Commander

24 December1944

What's Merry about all this, you ask? We're fighting - it's cold - we aren't home. All true but what has the proud Eagle Division accomplished with its worthy comrades of the 10th Armored Division, the 705th Tank Destroyer Battalion and all the rest? just this: We have stopped cold everything that has been thrown at us from the North, East, South and West. We have identifications from four German Panzer Divisions, two German Infantry Divisions and one German Parachute Division. These units, spearheading the last desperate German lunge, were headed straight west for key points when the Eagle Division was hurriedly ordered to stem the advance. How effectively this was done will be written in history; not alone in our Divisions glorious history but in World history. The Germans actually did surround us. their radios blared our doom. Their Commander demanded our surrender in the following impudent arrogance.

December 22nd 1944

To the U. S. A. Commander of the encircled town of Bastogne.

The fortune of war is changing. This time the U.S. A. forces in and near Bastogne have been encircled by strong German armored units. More German armored units have crossed the river Ourthe near Ortheuville, have taken Marche and reached St. Hubert by passing through HombresSibret-Tillet. Libramont is in German hands.

There is only one possibility to save the encircled U.S.A. Troops from total annihilation: that is the honorable surrender of the encircled town. In order to think it over a term of two hours will be granted beginning with the presentation of this note.

If this proposal should be rejected one German Artillery Corps and six heavy A. A. Battalions are ready to annihilate the U.S.A. Troops in and near Bastogne. The order for firing will be given immediately after this two hours term.

All the serious civilian losses caused by this Artillery fire would not correspond with the well known American humanity.

The German Commander

The German Commander received the following reply:

22 December 1944

To the German Commander:

NUTS!

The American Commander

Allied Troops are counterattacking in force. We continue to hold Bastogne. By holding Bastogne we assure the success of the Allied Armies. We know that our Division Commander, General Taylor, will say: Well Done!

We are giving our country and our loved ones at home a worthy Christmas present and being privileged to take part in this gallant feat of arms are truly making for ourselves a Merry Christmas.

A.C. McAuliffe

McAuliffe,

Commanding.

The first 2 weeks the company was mainly in a defensive posture repelling the odd attack. After the 4th Armored Division broke the siege the men of Easy Company and the entire 101st Airborne Division expected to be returned to Mourmelon, France but this didn't happen. The majority of the fighting for Easy Company came between December 30, 1944 and January 17, 1945 in the Foy/Noville area.

The company actually suffered very low casualties during the first 3 weeks with only one KIA, John Julian. One third of the non-combat casualties were from trench foot and frostbite. The company prides itself in the fact that not one man lowered himself to shooting himself in the foot or hand to get off the line. This was a common occurrence in some of the other companies.

On January 2, 1945 Easy Company and the rest of 2nd Battalion were on the move. The battalion was replaced in the Bois Jacques by 1st Battalion while 2nd Battalion prepared for what would become known as the 1000 yard attack.

The objective of the push was to cross the Bizory/Foy road to push the Germans out of the Bois des Corbeaux (3), the woods on the right side of the road as you face Foy. This is the attack when John Julian was killed.

The night of January 3, 1944 was when Easy Company was hit with an especially concentrated artillery attack. This was the night that Joe Toye and Bill Guarnere each lost a leg. According to Don Malarkey Joe Toye actually did ask, "Jesus, Malark, what does a man have to do to get killed around here?"

This was also the night when it's said that Buck Compton, one of Easy Company's best combat leaders, finally reached the limit of what he could take. He maintains that he did not leave the line voluntarily. He said it was strongly suggested by Col Sink not because of battle fatigue but because of trench foot. Shifty Powers seemed to confirm this. He said, "I think the man's feet just got to him. They were hurting him awful bad."

Buck Compton would later say that Winters was incorrect when said that he just walked off the line. Winters was in his command post and received the information second hand.

Compton said when he saw his good friends Guarnere and Toye lying on the ground he couldn't take it anymore. He considered Toye and Guarnere to be the toughest guys in the entire company. Compton, in an attempt to clarify the event said, "In truth I did not 'walk' of the line. I ran." He wasn't running because of a breakdown, he was running to the company command post, his only link to the battalion, to find Lt Dike to get a better idea of the situation.

Capt Winters would later say that Lt Compton made the mistake he warned his officers not to make. Capt Winters said the Lt Compton let himself become too friendly with the men. This meant that when these men were wounded it affected him more deeply.

Although this makes sense and there needs to be a separation between officer and enlisted Capt Winters blaming Lt Compton seems a little harsh. Winter's opinion that Compton failed in fulfilling his responsibilities as an officer also seems a little harsh. Capt Winters felt that an officer did not have the luxury to break down. An officer was supposed to be strong to give support to his men. Capt Winters saw Lt Compton's breakdown a sign of weakness.

Easy company along with the rest of the 506th PIR was replaced by the 501st PIR on January 4, 1944. The company went into regimental reserve in Luzery (4). Easy Company was placed back on the line January 9, 1944 to clear the woods west of Foy.

On January 10, 1945, while in the Fazone Woods (5) south of Recogne, Easy Company was again hit by a massive artillery attack. This is the night that Skip Muck and Alex Penkala were killed by a direct hit in their foxhole from an 88mm round. Not only did Easy Company lose two very good soldiers, some said they lost the heart and soul of the company in Skip Muck.

Earl McClung probably described the situation the best in only three words, "they just disappeared." All they were able to find were a few small pieces of flesh and sleeping bag. The shelling was so bad that night it became known as "The Night of Hell" by the men of Easy Company.

The unit maintained its defensive posture in the Bois Jacques and held the line until January 12, 1944 at 0900 when the attack on Foy (6) began.

The tension and stress of spending almost a month in the harsh conditions under constant bombardment showed itself as the men prepared to attack Foy. Buck Taylor came upon a German in a foxhole to his left. He instinctively shot him three times. Later he said that if he was thinking right he would have taken the man prisoner to send back to headquarters. They might have been able to get information about what they were up against in Foy.

Easy Company and Item Company from the 3rd Battalion made the attack on Foy. The rest of 2nd Battalion remained in reserve and provided suppressing fire for the advance. Easy Company attacked straight down from the Bois Jacques and

Item came from the left across the Bastogne-Foy road. They were able to secure Foy by 1100.

Lt Dike froze near a haystack during the approach to Foy. Dike stopped the entire company's attack when he became confused about the situation on the battlefield. He panicked because he lost sight of 1ˢᵗ platoon. Stopping in the middle of an open field left the men stationary targets, they were like fish in a barrel.

Capt Winters grabbed a rifle and started to head down to take command of Easy Company to get the unit moving again. He stopped himself reminding himself that he was responsible for the entire battalion not just Easy Company.

Winters knew he needed to get someone else to take the attack into Foy or Easy Company didn't stand a chance. Capt Winters turned to look for someone to send in to relieve Dike and he saw Lt Ronald Speirs. Dick Winters would later say that he did not select him "he was just there."

Lieutenant Speirs was the perfect man to take over Easy Company. He, like Winters, was able to quickly assess the situation and make quick and accurate decisions. Although some strongly disagreed with his leadership style, he used fear to control his men, he was dedicated and got the job done. Even though some of the men might have feared him they respected him for his command abilities and he was known as a man with almost no fear. He was a man who led from the front like a true leader. The most important thing to the men of Easy Company was that he was a man they knew they could trust.

The celebration for the capture of Foy was very short lived. The Germans counter attacked and by 0415 on the January 13, 1944 the Germans were able to retake the town. The German success was even shorter lived because Easy immediately counterattacked and captured the town for good by 0930.

An incident after the capture of Foy resulted in Capt Winter's dislike for the media reporters to grow even stronger. There was one reporter who faked a scene just to get a picture presenting him in a good light. While the men were evacuating the wounded the reporter pushed in to take one end of a stretcher. Of course he made sure he got blood on the sleeve of his coat to make it look like he was really doing his part.

Easy Company's next offensive was the assault on Noville, the high ground in the area, on the January 14, 1944. Capt Winters was concerned about the orders he received that meant his men would have to cross 2 km of open field in almost waist deep snow at high noon. The German's position gave them a perfect line of sight to see everything the Americans were doing around Foy and Recogne (7). Capt Winters knew that if he followed orders the men of 2nd Battalion would be sitting ducks.

Capt Winters surveyed the approach to Cobru (8) which is only about 800 meters from Noville (9) and noticed a deep ridge running up to the back side approach to Noville.

Instead of the straight ahead offensive Col Sink ordered Capt Winters opted to attack Recogne southwest of Noville and 1.4 km from Foy first. From there the attack advanced toward Cobru which is about 1.4 km from Recogne. The final attack on Noville began and first light on January 15, 1945 from Cobru which is only about 850 meters from Noville.

There was one portion of the plan that both Capt Winters as well as the rest of the 2nd Battalion were concerned about. The plan called for the unit's approach to Cobru to be single file in an exposed area. This left the men vulnerable to German gunfire.

Although this approach concerned Capt Winters he correctly reasoned that it was the best option for the attack. The snow was so deep that the advance would be difficult and extremely tiring. If the 2nd Battalion attack was spread out everyone would reach Cobru exhausted and not as effective. Advancing single file meant the men in the front would be tired but those behind them would benefit from the snow being packed down.

The reason Capt Winters opted for such a roundabout approach was to provide cover for his men. Once the men crossed the open area the ridge would afford some cover for the men as they approached from the southwest of Noville.

The Germans put up a stiff resistance in the defense of Noville but the battle was actually very short. The Germans realized that the American's next move after capturing Foy would be to take Noville and decided it would be better to drop back to set up a better line of defense. What the Americans encountered in Noville was a small rear guard that was only supposed to slow down the American's advance.

The men of 3rd Battalion were not as fortunate during their advance on Noville. Their commander, following orders, attacked straight up the middle toward the town leaving his men in the open, advancing up hill at high noon in snow that was waist deep in some places. The carnage Capt Winters saw inflicted on 3rd Battalion appalled him. He understood the need to obey orders but to sacrifice one's men in such a way just to follow orders went against everything he believed.

In later years Capt Winters would say the scene he witnessed that day reminded him of the scene in the movie Dr Zhivago where the army made a similar attack. There were bodies of the men from 3rd Battalion flying all over the place just like what happened in the movie.

Easy Company was supposed to go back to Mourmelon, France after this but the unit was again called on for one more offensive. They were sent to take Rachamps (10) and Hardigny. Each was simple and straight forward which is lucky because the men were completely exhausted by this time. These were the last offensives for Easy Company in Belgium. Their next test would be in Haguenau, France.

The unit spent its last night in a church in Rachamps before being shipped off to Haguenau. The sisters called in the local girl's choir to entertain the unit that night.

Easy Company went into Bastogne with 121 officers and soldiers. They received 24 replacements during their time in Belgium. When they left only 63 men remained in the company. The unit had suffered 85 casualties including 14 dead. To put this into perspective, a 50% casualty rate is considered to be horrific and Easy Company suffered a casualty rate of almost 58%.

Chapter 7 Easy Company Information

Easy Company was part of the 506th Parachute Infantry Regiment of the 101st Airborne Division. In August of 1942 Major General Bill Lee, the first commander of the division, briefed the men of the newly-formed unit. He told them, "The 101st Airborne Division has no history but it has a rendezvous with destiny." Maj Gen Lee was a father of the parachute infantry but never jumped into a combat situation. He had a heart attack just before D-Day and died June 25, 1948 at the age of 53. He was replaced by Maj Gen Maxwell Taylor, moved over from the 82nd Airborne Division. Maj Gen Taylor commanded the unit throughout the war.

I'm sure many of you have read the book or seen the miniseries about Easy Company. Both have caused a lot unwanted attention for many of the surviving members of Easy Company. The miniseries as well as the Ambrose book made the company seem like it was something special but none of the men considered themselves as being special nor do they consider themselves to be heroes. They are all just proud to do their part.

You have to remember there were many other companies like easy company and many other commanders like Capt Winters. The reason this story got told is because Steven Ambrose had the fame to get a publisher to release a book about a single company. This is something that other historians tried to do but were unable to do because the publishers didn't think anyone would be interested a book about a single company because it would be too limited in scope.

Before getting started let's look at a little side note that will help to stress the magnitude of the accomplishments of Easy Company and the entire 101st Airborne throughout its history.

As mentioned earlier the unit was ordered to remove its shoulder insignia before going to Bastogne. The simple fact that an elite force like the 101st Airborne Division would be defending the city forced a change in plans. The unit also had a very strong reputation with their German counterparts especially Col (Count) von der Heydte who was one of the German airborne commanders. His unit did a dance of death across Europe with the 101st Airborne starting at Carentan. He had the utmost respect for the men of the unit and even agreed to a meeting with Maj Winters after the release of the mini-series.

During Viet Nam all units were ordered to subdue their unit badges and the only exception was the Screaming Eagle of the 101st Airborne Division. The Vietnamese called them the Chicken Men because they didn't know what eagles were. The 101st Airborne Division was so feared and respected that even the sight of the Screaming Eagle was enough to change the tactics of the enemy. In fact, the normal tactic was to avoid them if possible. These are two examples of what Gen Bill Lee was talking about when he said the division "had a rendezvous with destiny".

The men of Easy Company were part of a group that would become known as "Citizen Soldiers." These were men who only enlisted to fight the Axis Powers in World War II. These men weren't even part of the regular army. They were part of what was called the Army of the United States. This was basically a conscription or draft force that, along with volunteers, was assembled to bolster the armed forces for the conflict.

Most of the men in Easy Company had no interest in making the army a career and less interest in the formalities of the army such as drill, inspections, and other "trivial" traditions. The only thing they cared about was killing Germans or Japanese.

There were a few men from Easy Company who had previous military experience. Some transferred in from other units. Joe Liebgott for instance was already a barber in the army. Others had ROTC experience. Bill Guarnere joined the Citizens Military Training Camp at Fort Meade in 1938. This is one reason he was put in charge of a platoon. Dick Winters was former enlisted and later got his commission because he felt he could do a much better job than some of the officers he had encountered.

There is a great story about Earl "One Lung" McClung. He is said to be one of the best combat soldiers in the war but probably the worst garrison soldier ever. The unit was scheduled for an inspection and of course McClung had no interest in such things. The other men in the company ironed his uniform, shined his shoes and got him ready for the inspection; everything went well so everyone was happy.

After the inspection was finished McClung went back into the barracks stripped of his uniform and threw it into the corner. The men still joke that the uniform is probably still in the corner where McClung threw it.

Easy Company was formed as part of an experiment at Camp Toccoa Georgia in July of 1942. The camp was originally called Camp General Robert Toombs after a confederate general. The camp had no permanent facilities until the paratroop school was established there.

Easy Company was part of a group that would become 101st Airborne Division. During that time they made sure to call themselves paratroops and not airborne because the airborne included the glider troops which the paratroops did not considered to be at the same level. Maj Gen Taylor, the 101st Airborne Division commander during the war, found out firsthand what it was like to be a glider troop. He went on a training mission after which he was said to have commented that the glider troops were even crazier than the paratroops and that he'd rather have a parachute any day.

The idea of the training program was to keep the entire group together during all phases of training then to deploy it together in combat. The military believed this would result in a more effective fighting force with improved cohesion which proved to be correct.

Easy Company along with Dog, Fox, and Headquarters companies made up the 2nd Battalion of the 506th PIR 101st Airborne Division. Easy Company was the special assault team of the battalion. They were meant to be similar to the Green Beret or Seals of today's military.

The airborne training, both the military and physical aspects, far exceeded what was required for the normal infantry soldier. The physical challenge was made even more difficult for Easy Company by the mandatory runs up and down the now famous Currahee Mountain.

The company's training was hard enough based on the army's requirements for the paratroops. Easy Company's was even more challenging because of the demands of Capt Sobel and Col Sink. The latter of the two men rewarded success by expecting greater success in the future.

The training was so hard that the career NCOs who were supposed to be conducting the physical training of the men were happy when Easy Company men got promoted to NCO. This meant that they could go back to the "normal" army where the demands weren't so high. Easy Company trained together for almost 2 years before they entered combat on June 6, 1944.

When their training was finished it was said that they knew each other so well that they could tell who a person was in the dark just by seeing his silhouette. They could recognize each other by the way the person wore his hat or by the way he stood.

Herb Suerth, a replacement who joined Easy Company right before Bastogne, gave a perfect example that stressed the level of training received. He said that when the trucks arrived in Bastogne the men jumped out of the truck, formed up and went out to scout the wooded area without receiving any orders.

Lynn "Buck" Compton mentioned in an interview that he was glad he was in the paratroops. They jumped in fought for a certain amount of time and then left. He said he wouldn't trade places with a regular infantryman and didn't know anybody who would.

With a couple of exceptions each man in the company was born between 1910 – 1928, children of depression. Although the men of Easy Company were from all over America the majority were either athletes or outdoorsmen. They were used to physical activities which helped during the demanding physical training and also helped in combat. Their competitive spirit made them want to be the best and fight with the best.

A great example of how the men's experience prior to the war paid off was when Shifty Powers spotted a tree from almost a mile away with no binoculars: "that hadn't been there before". Shifty, being taught to be alert to his surroundings, had already "memorized the line of foliage the day before."

He reported what he saw to First Sergeant Lipton who had a difficult time spotting what Shifty was talking about. Finally the tree moved and he was able to see, with binoculars, what Shifty was talking about. The Germans were placing trees in that area as part of an attempt to camouflage the buildup of 88mm anti-aircraft guns that were to be use to shoot down the C-47s as they attempted to resupply Bastogne.

This mountain boy from Virginia also proved to be the best shot in Easy Company. Some even argued that he was the best sharpshooter in the army. He honed his shooting skills by shooting first quarters, then knuckles, then pennies when they were thrown into the air. He said the only thing he couldn't hit was a dime.

There is another very interesting story about Cpl Earl "One Lung" McClung being able to smell Germans. When he was asked about it he said it wasn't the Germans he smelled. He said that the Germans wore so much leather that when it rained and the leather got wet he could smell the leather a mile away. No matter what he smelled, he was able to detect the enemy giving the men of Easy Company an upper hand during battle.

These are, of course, only two examples of how the heightened sensed of the outdoorsman proved to be valuable to the unit.

Another common thread that ran through the unit was the desire to fight with the best. These were men who excelled in what they did and wanted to fight alongside men with the same kind of drive. They wanted to be with men they could trust with their lives. In combat you have to be able to rely on the person to your right and left.

Each man, even men who feared death, was more than willing to give his life for his buddies. The fear of letting their friends down outweighed their fear of death. Babe Heffron tells a story that emphasizes this point very well. A friend of his, Jim Campbell, died when he advanced with Joe Toye after telling Babe to stay behind. He told Babe, "Heffron, you stay here with your gun, I'm going up". Babe continued trying to explain the anguish the event caused "…all your life ya gotta remember what one guy did because he did what he thought it was his job to do and he took a shot for you."

The almost psychotic determination not to go to the aid station after being wounded and the stories of men going AWOL from the hospital are true. After 90 days in the hospital the men would be reassigned to a different unit and none of the men of Easy Company wanted to leave his friends or fight with anyone else. Their loyalty to each other is probably why the group, with a few exceptions, has remained so close for so many years.

Even as hated as Capt Sobel, their first company commander was everyone even Maj Winters agree that the level of fitness and skill the men achieved was a direct result of the standards and training demanded by Capt Sobel. As Maj Winters would put it, the level of training wasn't the issue it was the approach Capt Sobel took in dealing with the men and the training.

One incident that testifies to the level of fitness achieved occurred during a 118 mile hike to Atlanta. Out of the entire 506th, only 3rd platoon from Easy Company made it the entire distance with no help.

Another testament to the training and quality of the men of Easy Company is that almost every person chosen to replace people at the battalion and regimental level was from Easy Company.

The men of Easy Company also share a strong conviction to the idea that they are not heroes. Every book this author has read and every documentary this author has seen reinforces this point.

When asked the men of Easy Company all say the real heroes are the men who didn't come back or those who were returned to the states to be buried. The common belief among the men is that heroes are the men who go above and beyond the call of duty.

In the eyes of the men in Easy Company there is no way to go more above and beyond than by giving your life for your friends and your country.

There are many of the men like Bill Guarnere who view the medics and chaplains as the real heroes. These were the men who seemed to be everywhere to help with total disregard for their own life. They rushed into the battle with their only weapon being medical supplies or a cross and Bible.

Those who are still alive almost 70 years later still grieve for those men who died so young. Their friends who had their lives end before they able to start living them, the men they consider heroes.

The men of Easy Company were pumped up and ready to go for their first jump into Normandy on D-Day. They were confident in their abilities and their training. They were confident that the army C-47 Skytrain pilots would get them where they need to go. They knew their objectives and what to do when they got there. They were ready.

After they returned from Normandy the experience there proved to be enough for them. After that they did what was necessary to the best of their abilities but the eagerness and excitement was gone. They no longer wanted to go into battle. They no longer wanted to be placed in the kill or be killed situation.

Each of the men of the company agrees that Bastogne was the most difficult time of the war. There are some who say they dread Christmas coming because of the memories the holiday stirs up from Bastogne.

J.B. Stokes commented in the documentary "We Stand Alone Together" made for the mini-series "Band of Brothers" that on cold nights he always tells his wife before they go to bed that he's glad he's not in Bastogne. For some they try to block out as much as possible but the memory of the bitter cold stays with them.

Many of the men commented about how seeing their friends being wounded bothered them at the time but they were also happy. The wound got them off the line and out of the war at least for a while. Some were lucky enough to get the "million dollar" wound that would get them back to America and out of the war completely. Capt Winters said that he noticed that the men who were killed seemed like they were finally at peace by the look on their face.

Joe Leniewski said that he didn't see the use in sitting down and crying when your friends got killed. The time for mourning and reflecting would come later. He is a devoted catholic and he still prays for his lost friends. He does remember that he gave up on praying after he jumped into Normandy because it didn't seem to do any good.

The idea of self inflicted wounds to get off the line wasn't unheard of even as determined as these men were to be there for their friends no matter what. Even Sgt Malarkey as strong as he was throughout the war thought about it. After Muck and Penkala were killed he thought about taking the easy way out. While standing around with some of the other guys he was holding his pistol inside his jacket, finger on the trigger, ready to take it out when he was startled from his thoughts. Later he thought that only a coward would do something like that.

Some men questioned if the wound that killed Cpl Hoobler on January 3, 1945 was really an accident. Even the type of gun he had can't be proven for sure. Sgt Malarkey says it was a .45 that Hoobler brought from the states. Stephen Ambrose identified it as a German luger, while Capt Winters said it was a Belgian .32.

For some who wanted off the line the solution was different. These were the ones who weren't able to shoot themselves to escape trials of Bastogne. This group of men decided to let Mother Nature help them out and they simply took their boots off and let their feet freeze. With the high number of cases of trench foot that resulted from the horrible conditions it was impossible to prove if the person did it on purpose or not.

The time the company spent in Bastogne left its mark on everyone. Some could not talk about their experiences there for many years. Others were able to openly discuss the events. Then there were people like Shifty Powers who would rather avoid the topic. Shifty just said, "Bastogne—I hate to talk about the place. It was a lot of fighting, just a lot of fighting."

Life after the war took the men of Easy Company to various parts of the U.S. Even with the many miles between them they remained very close. They started having reunions in 1947 that actually helped some men get over the trauma of combat. It has been noted that even those who were not physically wounded still bore the deep psychological and emotional scars of the experience. Don Malarkey said it took him 40 years to finally grieve and cry for the loss of his best friend Skip Muck.

The men of Easy Company also suffered the same feeling as many of the men who survived this war and other wars as well. After they got home they felt like they didn't belong anymore. They weren't the same people who they were before. They also suffered what's known as survivor's guilt. The feeling of "why did my friend die and I lived to return home".

Frank Soboleski avoided contact with the rest of the men for many years after the war. He refused to go the reunions even though he received an invitation every year. He told his wife he couldn't get the memories out of his head and didn't want to be around the other men. He wanted to work it out his own way. After several years of repeating his stance she basically asked "...and how's that working for you"? After he finally went to his first reunion he found that talking about the good times with his friends helped to get rid of the demons. He hasn't missed a reunion since.

Others like Floyd Talbert hit the bottle after the war and disappeared. He was finally found and made one reunion before succumbing to the effects of his drinking. Albert Blythe would also fall victim to the effects of alcohol in 1967 while still serving in the army. He just returned from a ceremony in remembrance of the Battle of the Bulge on December 11, 1967. He was admitted to the hospital with a perforated ulcer. He died on December 17, 1944, 23 years after the 101st Airborne Division deployed to Bastogne.

Cpl Earl McClung was so haunted by his demons he was not able to fit back into civilian life. He found himself constantly in fights for little or no reason. As a result he chose to go back into the army for 18 months and finally got the help needed to deal with the emotionally crippling memories of his time in Europe.

Each man had varying degrees of success in the civilian world. C. Carwood Lipton worked for an international glass company and Dick Winters eventually started his own animal food supply business. Both ended up in becoming fairly wealthy from their endeavors.

George Luz went home to Rhode Island where he worked as a maintenance consultant. Luz was well liked by everyone in the company and by people who met him after the war. He died on October 15, 1988 while repairing a commercial clothes dryer. As a testament to his character there were over 1500 people who attended his funeral.

Herbert Sobel carried his hatred for Easy to his grave. His obsession with "what the company did to me" resulted in his marriage failing and him becoming estranged from his kids.

He ignored attempts by Easy Company men to try to put the past behind. He never attended an Easy Company reunion even though he was invited each year.

In the late 1960s he attempted suicide by shooting himself in the head with a small caliber pistol. The attempt failed but the bullet passed just behind his eyes severing the optical nerve leaving him blind. He lived out the last 17 years of his life in an assisted living facility in Waukegan, Illinois. He died alone September 30, 1987. He was cremated and nobody attended his funeral.

There is much more information about many of the men of Easy Company in "From Toccoa to the Eagle's Nest: Discoveries in the Bootsteps of the Band of Brothers" by Dalton Einhorn. This book gives a good overview of the company from its beginning at Camp Toccoa through to the end of the war.

Additional Information

Easy Company was a special assault company which consisted of three 4 – 5 man platoons with three 12 man squads and a 9 man mortar squad along with Dog, Fox, and Company HQ formed the 2nd Battalion of the 506th Parachute Infantry Regiment. 1^{St}, 2nd, 3rd, and Battalion HQ together formed the entire 506th which consisted of the 4 battalions with a total for 3,000 – 4,000 men.

Perspective

There were 5800 men who volunteered to become paratroopers in the 506th PIR alone. Only 1948 made it through the training, of this group there were 140 assigned to Easy Company.

There were a total of 366 men who fought with the company during the war. The majority of these men came in the form of replacements.

The company had 49 men killed in action. The majority of the men were wounded with many of them being wounded more than once. One man, Joe Toye, was wounded 4 times including losing his right leg as a result of an artillery attack in Bastogne. He carried shrapnel from being wounded in Holland for the rest of his life. He also suffered nerve damage that made it difficult to use his right arm in later life.

Overall the company suffered 150 percent casualties. To put this into perspective, a 50% casualty rate is considered to be extremely bad.

Chapter 8 Easy Company - Training and Campaigns 1942-1944

July – November 1942: 506th activated at Camp Toccoa Georgia.

December 1942 through February 1943: Parachute and additional infantry training at Fort Benning Georgia.

February – May 1943: Training at Camp Mackall North Carolina as well as more training jumps.

June – August 1943: More training in Kentucky, Tennessee, and Fort Bragg North Carolina.

September 1943: Regiment moves to Camp Shanks New York and boards SS Samaria for trip to England. Regiment arrives in Swindon and then moves to Aldbourne.

September 1943 – May 1944: More training at Aldbourne. In May regiment moves to a marshalling area near Exeter then to Upottery Airfield from where it will depart for D-Day.

June 5, 1944: Regiment leaves Upottery with rest of force for jump on Normandy.

June 6, 1944: Regiment jumps around 0030.

June 7-8, 1944: Various battles in Normandy.

June 8 – 16, 1944: Battle for Carentan.

June 29, 1944: Company relieved and returns to Aldbourne.

September 17, 1944: Market Garden, Company jumps into Son Holland and advances to Eindhoven on its way to Arnhem. There are a series of intense battles along "Hell's Highway", the 19 mile stretch of road between Veghel and Grave, Holland throughout September.

October 3, 1944: Company is moved by truck from area around Eindhoven to an area between Waal and the Neder River which comes to be known as the "Island" There are more patrols and battles until the company is moved back to Mourmelon, France for rest and replacements.

December 17, 1944: Company sent to Bastogne and tasked with defending the Bois Jacques woods.

January 13 – 16, 1945: Company takes Foy, Noville, and Rachamps.

January 19 – February 25 1945: Company moved to Haguenau and fights along the Moder River.

March 1945: Company moved back to Mourmelon where the entire 101st Airborne Division is awarded the Presidential Unit Citation. It is the first time an entire division received the award.

April 1945: Company goes to Germany and finds concentration camps.

April 6 -10, 1945: Company moves to Kaprun Austria and begins occupation duties.

May 8, 1945: VE Day.

May – November 1945: High point men go home. The rest wait and train to ship out to Japan.

August 1945 – VJ Day war in Japan ends before this Easy is sent to the Pacific.

Easy Company's path took them to Normandy, Holland, Bastogne, Haguenau, the industrial Ruhr and other parts of Germany, and finally to Austria.

Chapter 9 Major Dick Winters

In an interview shortly before the miniseries debuted Winters said the war wasn't about individual heroics. He noted that men were able to do what they did because they became closer than brothers when faced with overwhelming hardships. They weren't out to save the world. They hated the blood, carnage, exhaustion and filth of war. The driving force was that they were horrified at the thought of letting down their buddies.

He always tried to get people to understand that success in war depends not on heroics but on bonding, character, getting the job done and "hanging tough," his lifelong motto. In combat, he wrote 50 years after the war, "your reward for a good job done is that you get the next tough mission."

Following the miniseries, Winters turned down most requests for interviews because he said he didn't want to appear like he was bragging. He was a very humble man and described as being furiously private.

When his friend author Larry Alexander asked if he could write his biography Winters approved. Alexander told Winters that he wanted to do the biography in the first person to emphasis his accomplishments. After Winters saw the first three chapters he was uncomfortable with the use of "I", and "Me", because it made it sound like he was the only one who was doing anything.

He did feel the story of Easy Company was an important one especially for young people. Because of this he was more likely to accept invitations to speak by local school groups and spent time with students at Cedar Crest High School, among others, than to talk to reporters. He was very sought after as a speaker and an example of his popularity was a talk he gave at Palmyra Middle School which attracted hundreds of spectators.

Even though he preferred to speak to the younger people he did agree to other speaking requests. Although his desire to go to war ebbed his support of the army did not. He willingly accepted invitations to speak at West Point on several occasions. The one topic that was always of interest was the capture of the gun battery at Brecourt Manor on D-Day. The approach he used is still taught as the official way to attack a fixed position.

People who knew Winters during and after the war said he is exactly what he appears to be. He could lead without ever raising his voice or swearing, although he did resort to these tactics when needed. His friend Bob Hoffman, a Lebanon, Pennsylvania architect, said Winters' eyes could "burn a hole right through you."

"The cohesion that existed in the company was hardly the result of my leadership," Winters wrote in "Beyond Band of Brothers" his 2006 memoir. "The company belonged to the men; the officers were merely the caretakers."

He said many times that his only regret from the war was he wasn't harder on his men. He felt that if he would have been harder on them then maybe a few more would have returned alive. It seemed that he blamed himself for the loss of his men. This shows he was as hard on himself as a leader as he was on his men.

Before his death in January 2011 he asked that his death not be announced until after the funeral. He knew the event would have turned into a media fiasco. He tried to avoid the media even in death.

Winter's men said he always lead from the front. When he said, "Let's go" he was in the lead. Bill Guarnere said, "He was never in the back. A leader personified."

Babe Heffron said, "He was one hell of a guy, one of the greatest soldiers I was ever under." Babe also said, "He was a wonderful officer, a wonderful leader. He had what you needed, guts and brains. He took care of his men, that's very important."

Robert "Burr" Smith, who fought with Easy Company as a sergeant and went on to command a Special Forces unit as part of the Delta force as a Lieutenant Colonel wrote a letter to Winters. In the letter he said, "I've soldiered most of my adult life. In that time I've met only a handful of great soldiers, and of that handful, only half or less come from my World War II experience, and two of them came from ol' Easy – you and Bill Guarnere."

Winter's described his view of leadership as:

> *"If you can, find that peace within yourself, that peace and quiet and confidence that you can pass on to others, so that they know that you are honest and you are fair and will help them, no matter what, when the chips are down."*

For all of his strengths Winters did seem to have one weakness; his inconsistency in dealing with issues concerning the men under his command. While he seemed to be very hard on some people, like Buck Compton, he overlooked problems of others. He was especially lenient with the alcohol problems of Capt Nixon and Lt Welsh.

He also seemed to have a strange idea of the seriousness of different situations. He punished Bill

Guarnere for bringing women to the house he was staying while the unit was in England; he felt Guarnere was taking advantage of his position. However; he did nothing when Guarnere shot two German POWs on D-Day.

Winters was especially harsh in his opinions of Maj Gen Taylor the commander of the 101st Airborne Division concerning his absence during the Battle of Bastogne. During an interview with Stephen Ambrose Winters blamed Taylor for being in Washington when the division was moved to Bastogne instead of being present to command the unit. Maj Gen Taylor was called to testify in Washington so he was following orders.

During the interview Ambrose pointed out that Winters wasn't really being fair in blaming Maj Gen Taylor for being in Washington since he was called there on official business. To this Winters tersely replied "I don't want to be fair." In his mind Maj Gen Taylor had failed in carrying out his obligations to the unit and nothing would change his mind.

The most telling aspect of Dick Winters leadership abilities is the fact that up till his death on January 2, 2011, almost 70 years after the war ended, was that he still commanded the same respect and admiration of the men of Easy Company as he did during the war.

He was a man who made quick, decisive, and accurate decisions in combat and this earned their admiration. Even though the war was over and the men were all civilians they still treated him almost like he was still their commander right to the end.

Stephen Ambrose was asked what made Winters so special in a television interview on August 12, 2001. Ambrose's replay was short and to the point,

> *"character, honesty, a firmness of purpose. Winters knows so much about weapons, about the men and what they can do and how to lead an attack. He knows what a good company commander needs to know."*

Dick Winters character can probably best be summed up in the quote that is used in the closing scene of the Band of Brothers. He quotes a letter from Bob Ranney when his grandson asked, "Grandpa were you a hero in the war? Grandpa said no...but I served with a company of heroes."

This was Dick Winters in the preverbal nut shell. He felt like he wasn't anything special and that he didn't do anything special. If he was approached by someone for an interview when "Sparky" Ron Speirs was present he would always tell them to talk with Sparky first. He felt that Speirs deserved more credit because he commanded the company for a longer period of time.

There is still a group that is pushing to get Winter's Distinguished Service Cross upgraded to the Medal of Honor. Anyone who understands Winters character will not be surprised to know that he never thought he deserved the Medal of Honor. He felt that he simply did what needed to be done.

Major Dick Winters' Obituary

PHILADELPHIA (AP) - Richard "Dick" Winters, the Easy Company commander whose World War II exploits were made famous by the book and television miniseries "Band of Brothers," died last week in central Pennsylvania. He was 92.

Winters died following a several-year battle with Parkinson's Disease, longtime family friend William Jackson said Monday.

An intensely private and humble man Winters had asked that news of his death be withheld until after his funeral, Jackson said. Winters lived in Hershey, Pa., but died in suburban Palmyra.

The men Winters led expressed their admiration for their company commander after learning of his death.

William Guarnere, 88, said what he remembers about Winters was "great leadership."

"When he said 'Let's go,' he was right in the front," Guarnere, who was called "Wild Bill" by his comrades, said Sunday night from his South Philadelphia home. "He was never in the back. A leader personified."

Another member of the unit living in Philadelphia, Edward Heffron, 87, said thinking about Winters brought a tear to his eye.

"He was one hell of a guy, one of the greatest soldiers I was ever under," said Heffron, who had the nickname "Babe" in the company. "He was a wonderful officer, a wonderful leader. He had what you needed, guts and brains. He took care of his men, that's very important."

Winters was born Jan. 21, 1918 and studied economics at Franklin & Marshall College before enlisting, according to a biography on the Penn State website. Winters became the leader of Company E, 506th Regiment, 101st Airborne Division on D-Day, after the death of the company commander during the invasion of Normandy.

During that invasion, Winters led 13 of his men in destroying an enemy battery and obtained a detailed map of German defenses along Utah Beach.

In September 1944, he led 20 men in a successful attack on a German force of 200 soldiers. Occupying the Bastogne area of Belgium at the time of the Battle of the Bulge, he and his men held their place until the Third Army broke through enemy lines, and Winters shortly afterward was promoted to major.

After returning home, Winters married his wife, Ethel, in May 1948, and trained infantry and Army Ranger units at Fort Dix during the Korean War. He started a company selling livestock feed to farmers, and he and his family eventually settled in a farmhouse in Hershey, Pa., where he retired.

Historian Stephen Ambrose interviewed Winters for the 1992 book "Band of Brothers," upon which the HBO miniseries that started airing in September 2001 was based. Winters himself published a memoir in 2006 entitled "Beyond Band of Brothers."

Two years ago, an exhibit devoted to Winters was dedicated at the Hershey-Derry Township Historical Society. Winters, in frail health in later years, has also been the subject of a campaign to raise money to erect a monument in his honor near the beaches of Normandy.

Winters talked about his view of leadership for an August 2004 article in American History Magazine:

"If you can," he wrote, *"find that peace within yourself, that peace and quiet and confidence that you can pass on to others, so that they know that you are honest and you are fair and will help them, no matter what, when the chips are down."*

When people asked whether he was a hero, he echoed the words of his World War II buddy, Mike Ranney: "No, but I served in a company of heroes."

"He was a good man, a very good man," Guarnere said. "I would follow him to hell and back. So would the men from E Company."

Arrangements for a public memorial service are pending.

Chapter 10 Key Players

Figure 46 Generalfeldmarshall Gerd von Rundstedt

Generalfeldmarshall Karl Rudolph Gerd von Rundstedt December 12, 1875 – February 24, 1953, was a key figure in the German army during WWII. He held some of the highest field commands during all phases of the war. He was sacked several times by Hitler because of disagreements but later returned to duty. He was brought back into service to take a figurehead position in charge of Army Group B and all forces in the West prior to the Battle of the Bulge. Feldmarshall Walter Model was actually the commander of Army Group B. Hitler hoped the idea of the older, more defensive minded von Rundstedt being in charge would lull the allies into a more relaxed state of defense, it worked.

Von Rundstedt was charged with war crimes after the war but never stood trial because of poor health. He was released from captivity in 1948 and lived in Hanover until his death.

Figure 47 Feldmarshall Walter Model

Feldmarshall Otto Moritz Walter Model January 24, 1891 – April 21, 1944 was one of Hitler's favorites and an ardent Nazi. Model was known as a very aggressive, offensive minded leader so the Germans tried to hide his participation in the command of the west during the build up for the Ardennes offensive. He was the commander of Armee Group B, all the forces that participated in the offensive.

Model acquired his aggressive reputation during the time he spent on the Eastern front and he was very good at what he did. It wasn't until he was moved to the west and foiled the Allied plans during

Operation Market Garden that Model's true calling came out. He became known as Hitler's "Fireman" because of his ability to quickly analyze a situation and throw together a quick effective defense.

Model's defensive abilities played a major role in the failure of Market Garden and were instrumental in the horrific losses the Americans suffered in the Hütgenwald.

Model was a typical yes man supporting Hitler's every decision. That is until Wacht am Rhein. He sarcastically said that ALL he has to do is to attack through the Ardennes and push through to Antwerp in three days during December, January, and February, the worst three months of the year.

Near the end of the war Model realized there was no hope for victory so on April 21, 1944 he asked his intelligence officer to shoot him but the major refused. Model was worried that the Russians would capture him and he lived by the rule that Feldmarshalls do not become prisoners.

When his intelligence officer refused to shoot him Model put the gun to his head and shot himself. His body was moved from place-to-place to hide it from the Russians. Finally, when his son felt it was safe, he was buried in the military cemetery near Vossenack, Germany in plot 1074.

Figure 48 General of the Panzer Armee Hasso Eccard Friherr von Manteuffel

General of the Panzer Armee Hasso Eccard Freiherr von Manteuffel, January 14, 1897 – September 24, 1978, was a major architect of Operation Wacht am Rhein or Watch on the Rhein. The operation was designed to look like a defensive build up to fool the allies. Von Manteuffel preferred a more defensive and smaller scale operation like von Rundstedt but he was over-ruled by Hitler.

Von Manteuffel was promoted to the grade of General on September 1, 1944 so he could take

command of the 5th SS Panzer Armee that was
responsible for the push through the center of the
offensive toward the city of Bastogne.

Von Manteuffel is one of only 27 men who
were awarded the Knight's Cross with Oak Leaves,
Swords, and Diamonds. He was the only leader of his
rank in the Wehrmacht to receive the award. This was
the highest award presented by the Third Reich.

He was elected to parliament after the war
and supported rearmament. He was responsible for
the re-naming of the German military from the
Wehrmacht to the Bundeswehr.

Baron von Manteuffel was also to become
very good friends with Guy Franz Arend who opened
the first museum in Bastogne to commemorate the
battle. The Baron felt it was important for the story to
be told from both sides so everyone would
understand what happened.

Figure 49 General Heinrich Diepold Georg Freiherr von Lüttwitz

General Heinrich Diepold Georg Freiherr von Lüttwitz December 6, 1896 – October 9, 1969 was a panzer commander during WWII. He was a decorated officer including the Knight's Cross of the Iron Cross with Oak Leaves and Swords.

General Lüttwitz was the commander of the XLVII Corps during the Battle of the Bulge. He was in command of the forces that attacked at the center of the advance. He was the one who requested McAuliffe's surrender and was not amused with the reply he received. He does have the distinction of having his 2nd Panzer Division being the unit that pushed the furthest into Belgium.

Figure 50 Major General Meinrad von Lauchert

Major General Meinrad von Lauchert, August 29, 1905 – December 4, 1987, entered active duty on 24 April 1924 as an Officer Cadet. He advanced to the rank of Captain by the beginning of World War II and was promoted to Battalion Commander the first day of the attack on Poland in 1939.

Von Lauchert served with the 39th Panzer Regiment of the 4th Panzer division throughout the Polish and French operations. He was a member of the first push into Russia during Operation Barbarossa and received the Knights Cross and Iron Cross.

He was put in command of the 2nd Panzer Division under von Manteuffel's 5th Panzer Armee the day before the Battle of the Bulge kicked off. Although he was new with the division his unit was able to push further into Belgium than any other German unit. His unit finally ran out of gas in Celles just a few kilometers from the Meuse River.

Figure 51 Brigadier General Anthony McAuliffe

Brigadier General Anthony Clement McAuliffe, July 2, 1898 – August 11, 1973, was the commanding general in Bastogne during the Battle of the Bulge. He was told by Maj Gen Troy Middleton to hold Bastogne at all costs. He is famous for providing what is probably the most well known reply to a surrender request in history: NUTS!.

McAuliffe graduated from West Point in November 1918. He served in several administrative positions prior to joining the 101st Airborne Division.

Once with the airborne McAuliffe commanded the division artillery from the time the unit jumped on D-Day.

After the Battle of the Bulge, McAuliffe was given command of the 103rd Infantry Division of the US 7TH Army. He held the command from January 15, 1945 to July 1945.

After the war McAuliffe remained in the army serving in many different positions. He returned to Europe in 1953 as the commander of the 7th Army and would eventually be the commander of the United States Army Europe.

Figure 52 Lieutenant General George S. Patton Jr

Lieutenant General George Smith Patton Jr, November 11, 1885 – December 21, 1945 was a graduate of West Point and earned fame as a commander during World War II.

Despite all his bravado, probably a cover, Patton was actually a very insecure man. He even wrote to his wife that he would never be anything more than a mediocre platoon leader. Many people feel that this is what drove him to succeed.

Patton was a hard but fair leader. He was the only general who took his entire staff with him from one assignment to the next.

Patton was a true paradox. It's just impossible to figure him out. He was arrogant but humble, hard but sympathetic, cruel but kind. One thing is for sure, he's the kind of leader the Americans needed at the time.

Patton fought in many theaters during World War II including Sicily and France. He almost caused a premature end to his career when he slapped a soldier suffering from battle fatigue and accused him of being a coward. Only his friendship with General Eisenhower saved his career.

Patton served as a figurehead commander of a mostly fictitious First United States Army Group (FUSAG), part of Operation Fortitude, during the preparation for D-Day. He finally entered the fighting in France in August entering the continent at Cherbourg.

During the Battle of the Bulge Patton quickly moved his army from fighting in a sector to the south and moved over 100 hours in just 4 days to relieve the siege.

Patton died as the result of injuries he received in a car accident just after the war ended. He is buried in the Luxembourg Cemetery.

Colonel William L. Roberts (September 18, 1890) Col Roberts was the commander of armored units during WWII. He was a graduate of West Point Military Academy, class of 1913. Roberts rose up the ranks of the U.S. Army where in 1940 he became a professor of military science and tactics at the Citadel in Charleston, South Carolina. He was in the 20th Armored Division before being assigned to the 10th Armored Division in 1943. He was the commanding officer of Combat Command B when the 10th Armored Division landed in Europe and continued until Brig. Gen. Edwin Piburn took command from November 5, 1944 until the Battle of the Bulge began on December 16, 1944.

(Information on Col Roberts courtesy of Martin King)

Figure 53 Capt Richard D. "Dick" Winters

Major Richard D. "Dick" Winters (January 21, 1918 – January 2, 2011) was a decorated war veteran during WWII. He commanded Easy Company, 506th PIR, 101st Airborne Division starting on D-Day until Operation Market Garden when he was promoted to battalion to replace the battalion executive officer. He led the attack at Brecourt Manor on D-Day destroying the enemy 105 mm howitzers there saving many allied lives on Omaha and Utah Beaches.

Winters decided to become an officer when he attended a training session on a specific weapon. The officer who was conducting the class not only had the wrong manual but the weapon he had was not even the one being discussed. He felt he could do better and put in for a commission.

He was said to be a quiet man and seldom raised his voice or used foul language. He had a way of getting his point across and the men were more than willing to follow him. Although he was not loud or boisterous it is said he could burn a hole through you with a glare.

After World War II he was reactivated to go to Korea. If he had to go fight he decided like in World War II he wanted to fight with the best so he volunteered to go into the Rangers. He was assigned to train and evaluate the Ranges but his superiors did not go with the men and did not want him to go when the trainees went into the field.

This confused Winters because he felt the men could not be properly evaluated unless someone went with them. He finally got permission to accompany a group of trainees and they were impressed with his physical and tactical abilities. His superiors were less impressed because his going with the group and making such a strong impression made them look bad.

He wrote a letter requesting that he be granted a waiver from going to fight in Korea. The waiver was disapproved and he served as a training officer for a short time. He was scheduled to go to Korea and was awaiting departure when someone came in the room where he was waiting with a group of other men. They were told that any officer who was recalled involuntarily was free to leave. He didn't hesitate; he got up and left. His out-processing was complete and he was out of the army again that same day.

A colonel tried to stop Winters from leaving. He told Winters that he was being foolish by not staying in the army. The colonel pointed out that with his military record he could have a good career in the army.

Winters reply was simple but to the point. He replied to the colonel; "If you keep sending me out where people are shooting at me, I'm not going to have much of a career in anything, and I'm surely not going to enjoy my retirement."

After the discussion he went to pick up his separation pay and that was the end of his military service. He went back home to Pennsylvania where he lived the rest of his life in peace as he promised himself and God; until the Band of Brothers was released.

Chapter 11 More Information

Although the following has nothing to do with the Band of Brothers directly I feel it's important and needs to be shared because it is important to the Battle of Bastogne.

This author found some information that is a little disturbing. It's not the information actually it's that fact that the information does not seem to be widely disseminated. While reading the obituaries in a newspaper this author read about Jake McNiece a member of a demolition team called the Filthy 13. The group played what seems to be a significant role in the resupply of Bastogne and should be given credit.

Jake McNiece was one of the founding members of a group nicknamed the Filthy 13. This group was a special regimental demolition team from the 506th PIR, 101st Airborne Division. They made many dangerous jumps but many of the history books remain silent about their accomplishments.

The group got the name the Filthy 13 because they did not like to bathe, shave, or change their uniforms. If they couldn't find anyone else to fight with they got drunk and fought amongst themselves. It wasn't uncommon for someone to have to bail them out of jail for them to go on a mission.

McNiece liked to say that the movie the Dirty Dozen is based loosely on the group. The difference between the real and fictional characters is that none of the Filthy 13 was a convict. However; they did spend their fair share of time in jail. Jake McNiece was just getting out of jail for being AWOL when he was told about the jump into Bastogne.

The most common story told about the resupply at Bastogne is centered around the weather clearing so that the C-47s could hit their drop zones. What is not often told is that the Filthy 13 jumped into Bastogne as pathfinders early in the morning that the drop was made.

The insertion of the Filthy 13 was actually attempted twice. The first attempt was on December 22, 1944. The men were notified that they would be making a combat drop but were given no other information. When Jake McNiece, the informal leader of the group, asked when he would be briefed he was told he would have to wait until he was on the airplane.

When they were briefed the information was very limited. Nobody was even sure of the status of the 101ˢᵗ Airborne Division since there were no communications with the unit for 2 days. To make the drop the pilot was supposed to fly 400 miles and find a spot on the map about 2 miles in diameter, no problem, or so it would seem.

The catch was that the C-47 that was supposed to take the men to Bastogne had no navigational equipment and no instruments. The aircrew figured that they were approximately 35 miles past Bastogne before they realized they missed the target.

The drop was tried again on the morning of December 23, 1944 with a new plane and a "crackerjack" pilot who was guaranteed to get them to Bastogne. The landmark used for identifying Bastogne was the graveyard across from the Bastogne Barracks. When Jake McNiece saw the graveyard he was sure it was Bastogne because of the size of the graveyard. The men jumped and landed near the area manned by Charlie Company.

After arriving in Bastogne the Filthy 13 set up 4 each CM-4 panels, their Eureka antennas, and infrared lights to guide the C-47s to the drop zone. They set up one of the antenna on the top of a pile of bricks just to get it higher in the air. The set up was successful and within less than 4 hours there were 244 C-47s approaching Bastogne with more than 322 tons of badly needed supplies.

Pathfinders Setting up Eureka Antenna on Pile of Bricks

After the jump the men of the Filthy 13 stayed in Bastogne and fought with the 506th PIR through the rest of the battle.

Another fact that is often omitted is that a group of 5 doctors and 4 medical technicians volunteered to go into Bastogne via glider. Lt Gen Maxwell Taylor, commander of the 101st Airborne Division, said himself that he'd rather jump in using a parachute than to go in by glider. This didn't seem to bother the medical team. Dr Lamar Soutter the leader of the group later said, "This was something we felt we absolutely had to do."

The medical team flew into Bastogne on December 26, 1944 along with 10 other gliders containing almost 3,000 gallons of 80 octane fuel. Although this was an especially hazardous mission all the gliders landed without incident.

This author discussed these omissions with other historians to get their take on the matter. Most of them, being historians, said that maybe each is just the one fact too far. It is true that getting down to activities that included groups this small are not usually discussed in books but these seem significant enough to include in this book especially since it is about Bastogne, just a small, but very significant, part of the overall battle.

Chapter 12 GPS Addresses and Making Maps with Google Maps

The following is the GPS information for those of you who would like to program the sites, memorials, and museums into your GPS. There is also information on how you can use the GPS information to make maps using Google Maps for those of you who would rather have paper in hand. It would also be helpful if you go to the Information Center in Bastogne to get a city map.

The following is a list of the sites, memorials, and museums with the corresponding GPS address. This list includes where to find the foxholes in the woods. You should be able to take your GPS out of your car to help you find the foxholes. You can do the same thing during your walk through Bastogne. The coordinates are separated by a comma. The first coordinate is north/south and the second is east/west. You can put the coordinates just like they appear into Google to do your search.

Information Center	50.000831,5.714792
10th Armored Division Command Post	50.001298,5.713861

Renee` Lemaire Plaque	49.999826,5.714328
101st Airborne Museum	49.999143,5.712096
Pays d'Ardenne Museum	49.999826,5.714328
Patton Memorial	49.998321,5.715481
St James Church	50.005143,5.721167
Memorial to WWI/WWII	50.005432,5.721948
101st Aid Station Entrance	50.006536,5.721049
101st Command Post	50.00818,5.718394
Cady Memorial	50.008825,5.731405
10th Armored Memorial	50.008553,5.729315
Bastogne Military Museum/	50.010528,5.734664
Mardasson Memorial	
Woods of Peace	50.022937,5.762106
Easy Company Memorial	50.028848,5.756527
Entrance to Foxholes	50.033336,5.752987
Sniper House in Foy	50.044409,5.749379
Temporary Cemetery	50.049174,5.743972
German Cemetery	50.049389,5.741187
American Indian Memorial	50.045157,5.732312
Turn to Noville	50.051945,5.736469
Rachamps Church	50.083568,5.787853
Glessener Memorial	49.995009,5.706407
Turn to Pillbox	49.987587,5.69424
Pillbox	49.983558,5.698982

To make maps with Google Maps is very easy. First open Google and click on the Maps option. When the window opens put the GPS coordinates for where you are starting in the search field and hit return. This will show the location of that place on the map.

Next click on the Get Directions button at the top left. Click on the double arrows at the right of the search fields to move the starting point to the top. Now copy and paste the GPS address for the site, memorial, or museum you want to visit into the bottom search field and click on the GET DIRECTIONS button.

This will display a map along with the directions on how to get to the location. Click the printer icon and click on the box for Include large map located at the top center of the window if you want a map included then click the Print button.

To change from location to location simply make sure the from GPS address is in the top search field and the to GPS address is in the lower search field. Make sure to resize the map if needed if you want to print the map.

Epilogue

Just like the events leading up to the Battle of the Bulge and the Battle of Bastogne played a role in how the battle unfolded the battle itself played a significant role in the rest of the war. The Germans suffered huge losses in both manpower and equipment during the battle. This coupled with the increasing success of the Allied bombing campaigns reducing the German's manufacturing capabilities meant that the Germans were never to mount another major offensive during the rest of the war.

It must be pointed out that there was a second German offensive during the same period, Operation Northwind from December 21, 1944 – January 25, 1945, which was an attempt to break through the thinly spread American 7th Army and 1st French Free Army in the Alsace area along a 110 Km (68 mile) front. It was hoped that this offensive could provide the breakout Hitler wanted or at least relieve pressure from the units still fighting in the Ardennes region. Although this offensive was fought in a separate area the casualty total for the Battle of the Bulge, for the Germans, includes the casualties for Operation Northwind.

The Battle of the Hurtgen Forest mentioned in the Prologue finally took a turn in the favor of the allies because of the depletion of forces and equipment as a result of the battle. After slugging it out with the Germans from around mid September 1944 the Americans were finally able to advance past the Schnee Eifel in February 1945.

The end of the Battle of the Bulge also signaled an end to the stalemate in the area where Operation Market Garden took place. The British were finally able to push over the Lower Rhein and into the German industrial heartland in the Ruhr Valley area.

The Germans would put up a determined fight for the rest of the war but after the Battle of the Bulge the war was all but over. Germany's great fighting force was all but gone. In its place were young kids, old men, and conscripts from captured nations who really didn't want to have any part of the war.

On March 15, 1945 the 101st Airborne Division was the first full division to receive the Presidential Unit Citation as the result of the unit's gallant stand in Bastogne. Although each unit is not individually named the citation reads: "The 101st Airborne Division and attached units."

In January 1945 BG McAuliffe was given command of the 103rd Infantry Division. He was in command of the unit when it broke through the

Siegfried Line and pushed through Germany to link up with the American 5th Army coming up from Italy.

Not everyone in command faired so well in the aftermath of the Battle of the Bulge. Field Marshal Montgomery caused a huge outcry when he held a press conference on January 7, 1945 where he took credit for stopping the Germans. He claimed that the only reason the Americans weren't defeated on the northern shoulder was that he was brought into command.

This is an extremely bold statement since he sat on the opposite side of the Meuse River while the Americans took the brunt of the offensive. He also failed to point out that he was only placed in command temporarily and only because Lt Gen Bradly had difficulty maintaining communication with the forces on the northern shoulder. Needless to say, there was a very strong outcry for him to be sacked. It is possible that he was using this perceived "saving of the day" to gain a little credibility back since the failure of Operation Market Garden.

It is said that the Americans were successful in slowing the Germans down in the initial stages because of their ability to make things up as they went. They were able to fall back and set up what is known as a defense in depth. This means you hold strategic points and do not try to establish a defensive line. This is not a tactic that is actually taught but the men realized this was their best option for success.

Another factor that played in the American's favor was the German's miscalculation on how long it would take to rebuild the bridge at Dasburg where the 5th Panzer Armee crossed in the center of the attack toward Bastogne.

The Germans estimated it would take 3-4 hours to rebuild the bridge and it actually took 7-8 hours. Add to this the poor condition of the roads caused by Allied bombing and the poor road conditions the Germans were behind from the very start. But the most unusual stalling point was in the form of a gate. This gate was across the road and nobody knew where to find the key. Instead of destroying the gate the 5th Panzer Armee had to wait until the key could be found and the gate unlocked.

It's been said that the American GI of the time only did what was necessary, no more – no less. In his book "Battle: The Story of the Bulge" John Toland explained how the American GI was transformed during this battle. Many went from "I have nothing against the Germans, they never did anything to me" to a view of wanting to kill every German they found. The offensive turned the normal American soldier into a determined almost callous fighting machine.

This was the one factor that the Germans could not anticipate or control. Even units that were pinned down with essentially no hope of surviving refused to withdraw. Many were killed or captured but these men held their ground giving the airborne and other units rushing to the area time to arrive.

A major factor for success in many of these cases was the leadership. This not only applied to the officers but the noncommissioned officers as well. The men, in most cases, felt that they were being lead into battle and not just being sent to the front to die. It is much easier to motivate men when they feel they are being taken care of by a good, honest, reliable leader.

Conclusion

There were many consequences that stemmed from the Ardennes offensive. The fallout hit both sides but the Germans were hit the hardest. The loss of men and material could never be recuperated. The losses during the battle weren't the only ones suffered by the Germans. The Germans also lost many of their troops and much of their equipment when some of their former allied countries changed sides and fought for the allies after the defeat in the Ardennes.

To compound Germany's situation, Hitler made one last ditch attempt to slow the American's counter offensive during the later stages of the battle by trying to deal a crippling blow against the Allied Air Forces. The Luftwaffe launched a surprise attack of over 1,100 aircraft to destroy as many aircraft and airfields as possible.

The attack was a success in one aspect because it lifted the moral of the soldiers if only for a brief time. The aircraft, many flown by men with only a few hours of flying experience, approached at tree top level thus avoiding allied radar. The raid did destroy many aircraft in the air and on the ground and also damage some airfields but the loss of men and aircraft was devastating to the German air corps. As a result of losses of aircraft and pilots the Germans were never able to mount another serious threat to the allied aircraft for the rest of the war.

This was the point where many of the German soldiers who felt that Germany still had a chance to win the war realized there was no longer any hope for victory. Many of the German soldiers captured as the Americans pushed the Germans out of the bulge were asked why they fought so hard knowing there was no way for them to win. The common answer was family.

The German units were normally put on the line together and not relieved so they fought together continually. This long period of time living in the face of death bonded them closer than family. They fought to protect their friends just like the men of Easy Company.

The Battle of Bastogne is remembered as a glowing example of the American fighting spirit and determination. None of the men trapped in Bastogne thought of surrender or withdrawal. Neither of these choices was an option. But this was not the only example of almost superhuman dedication during the Battle of the Bulge.

There were other units that fought just as bravely with the only difference being they didn't get the headlines. These were the units that fought in places like the Schnee Eifel, St Vith, Wiltz, Clervaux, and what is known as the Fortified Goose Egg. These men faced many of the same challenges as the men in Bastogne. These men were just as determined and fought until there was no longer a hope to hold out in most cases. Most had to be ordered to withdraw and only did it then because they had no other choice.

Even when withdrawal was necessary there were still men who wanted to stay and fight. Gen Gavin, commander of the 82nd Airborne Division, was told by Montgomery that he had to withdraw to "tidy up" the line. The idea of being ordered to retreat made Gen Gavin furious. He said the 82nd Airborne Division never retreated and it would not start then. Gavin lost the argument and the 82nd Airborne Division was forced to withdraw.

Stories of the courage and dedication in the face of overwhelming odds seemed to be on the front pages of every newspaper in the world. Well, almost every newspaper. In England the major story during the battle was the terrible reality that there would not be enough beer in some parts of the country to last over the holidays.

General Bruce C. Clarke commander of Combat Command B, 7th Armored Division said the Ardennes offensive was… "the greatest American Battle of the Second World War. The American Army suffered 80,000 casualties. The German offensive stopped the American progress and took away their opportunity to reach Berlin before the Russians." To him, the Russians getting to Berlin first this was the most significant consequence of the battle.

Appendix 1 Unit Strengths

Army Group – 400,000 or more with several Armies typically commanded by a full General

Army – 50,000 or more with several Corps typically commanded by a Lieutenant General

Corps – 20,000 to 45,000 with 2 – 5 divisions typically commanded by a Lieutenant General

Division – 10,000 to 15,000 with 3 brigade sized elements typically commanded by a Major General

Brigade – 3,000 to 5,000 with 2 – 5 divisions typically commanded by a Colonel

Battalion – 300 to 1,000 with 4 – 6 companies typically commanded by a Lieutenant Colonel

Company – 62 to 190 with 3 – 5 platoons typically commanded by a Captain

Platoon – 16 to 44 typically commanded by a lieutenant with an NCO as second in command

Squad – 9 to 10 typically commanded by a Sergeant or Staff Sergeant

Appendix 2 Military Abbreviations

A.A. – Anti Aircraft; Weapons used to shoot down aircraft.

AWOL – Absent Without Leave

CC – Combat Command; A major tactical unit made up of a headquarters, headquarters company and attached units such as armor, infantry, and artillery.

D-Day – A generic term to mark the beginning of a military operation. Since the landings on June 6, 1944 it has been directly connected to this event.

GI – American Soldier

KIA – Killed in Action

MLR – Major Line of Resistance

NCO – Noncommissioned Officer, sergeants and corporals in the grade of E-3 and above.

PIR – Parachute Infantry Regiment

POW – Prisoner of War

ROTC – Reserve Officers' Training Corps

R&R – Rest and Relaxation

SNAFU – Situation Normal All Fouled Up

VE Day – Victory in Europe

VG – Volksgrenadier – German infantry made up of individuals who would normally not qualify to serve because of age, physical requirements, or other issues.

VJ Day – Victory in Japan

Appendix 3 American Army Rank Structure

Officers

General of the Army – Five Stars

General (Gen) – Four Stars

Lieutenant General (Lt Gen) – Three Stars

Major General (Maj Gen) – Two Stars

Brigadier General (BG) – 1 Star

Colonel (Col) – Eagle

Lieutenant Colonel (Lt Col) – Silver Oak Leaf

Major (Maj) – Gold Oak Leaf

Captain (Capt) – Two Silver Bars

1st Lieutenant (1Lt) – One Silver Bar

2nd Lieutenant (2Lt) – One Gold Bar

Enlisted 1942 - 1948

E-7 Master Sergeant (M/Sgt) – Six Stripes

E-7 First Sergeant (F/Sgt) – Six Stripes with a Diamond in the center

E-6 Technical Sergeant (T/Sgt) – Five Stripes

E-5 Staff Sergeant (S/Sgt) – Four Stripes

E-5 Technician Third Grade (T/3) – Four Stripes with a T

E-4 Sergeant (Sgt) – Three Stripes

E-4 Technician Fourth Grade (T/4) – Three Stripes with a T

E-3 Corporal (Cpl) – Two Stripes

E-3 Technician Fifth Grade (T/5) – Two Stripes with a T

E-2 Private First Class (Pfc) – One Stripe

E-1 Private – No Insignia (Pvt)

Technicians were addressed as the equivalent grade. A T/3 would be referred to as Staff Sergeant. Technicians did not normally have the authority to issue orders unless specifically granted the authority by an NCO.

Appendix 4 German Army Rank Structure

Officers

American Equivalent

Leutnant	2nd Lieutenant
Oberleutnant	1st Lieutenant
Hauptmann	Captain
Major	Major
Obersleutnant	Lieutenant Colonel
Oberst	Colonel
Generalmajor	Brigadier General
Generalleutnant	Major General
General	Lieutenant General
Generaloberst	General
Generalfeldmarshall	General of the Army

The Germans also had variations for different positions but this is the basic rank structure.

Enlisted

	American Equivalent
Obersoldat	Private
Gefreiter	Private First Class
Unteroffizier	Corporal
Unterfeldwebel	Sergeant
Feldwebel	Staff Sergeant
Oberfeldwebel	Master Sergeant
Stabsfeldwebel	Sergeant Major

The enlisted grades also had some special ranks for specific positions. This is the basic rank structure.

Appendix 5 German SS Rank Structure

Officers

Untersturmführer	2nd Lieutenant
Obersturmführer	1st Lieutenant
Hauptsturmführer	Captain
Sturmbannführer	Major
Obersturmbannführer	Lieutenant Colonel
Standartenführer	Colonel
Brigadeführer	Brigadier General
Gruppenführer	Major General
Obergruppenführer	Lieutenant General
Oberstgruppenführer	General
Reichsführer-SS	General of the Army

In the SS the Führer designation simply meant leader just like the case of Hitler himself. Although the SS had officer ranks the separation between the officer and enlisted corps wasn't as strict. The men were bound by duty and would follow orders as necessary.

SS Enlisted

	American Equivalent
Schütze	Private
Sturmmann	Private First Class
Rottenführer	Corporal
Untersharführer	Sergeant
Sharführer	Staff Sergeant
Obersharführer	Sergeant First Class
Hauptsharführer	Master Sergeant
Sturmsharführer	Sergeant Major

There were a couple of different ranks in the administration portion of the SS. These are the enlisted ranks for the Waffen (armed) SS the portion of the SS that fought during the war.

Appendix 6 American Forces at Bastogne

101st Airborne

501st Parachute Infantry Regiment

502nd Parachute Infantry Regiment

506th Parachute Infantry Regiment

327th Glider Infantry Regiment

321st Glider Infantry Regiment

907th Glider Field Artillery Battalion

377th Parachute Field Artillery Battalion

463rd Parachute Field Artillery Battalion

81st Airborne Anti-Aircraft Battalion

326th Airborne Engineer Battalion

101st Airborne Signal Company

801st Airborne Ordinance Maintenance Company

326th Airborne Medical Company

426th Airborne Quartermaster Company

Attached Units

3rd Army, 10th Armored Division, CC B

    Team O'Hara

    Team Cherry

    Team Desobry

    705th Tank Destroyer Battalion

    755th Field Artillery Battalion

    333rd Field Artillery Battalion

    969th Field Artillery Battalion

    109th Field Artillery Battalion

    771st Field Artillery Battalion

    687th Field Artillery Battalion

    158th Engineer Battalion

    420th Armored Artillery Battalion

    73rd Armored Artillery Battalion

    9th Armored Engineer Battalion, Company C

    80th Armored Medical Battalion, part of Company B

Team SNAFU: This group consisted of soldiers who were retreating from the front. The main composition of the group was from the 28th Infantry Division and Combat Command R of the 9th Armored Division.

Appendix 7 German Forces at Bastogne

LXVI Infantry Corps

18th Volksgrenadier Division

62nd Volksgrenadier Division

LVIII Armored Corps

506th Volksgrenadier Division

116th Panzer Division (Windhund)

XXXVII Armored Corps

2nd Panzer Division

Panzer Lehr

26th Volksgrenadier Division

Führer-Begleit – Führer Escort Brigade

Appendix 8 Recommendation for Award for Renee Lemaire

Medical Detachment
20th Armored Infantry Battalion
APO 260, US Army
1 January 1945

SUBJECT: Commendation for Renee Bernadette
Emilie Lemaire (deceased)
To: Commanding General
10th Armored Division
APO 260, US Army
(Attn: Division Surgeon)

Thru Channels:

As Battalion Surgeon, 20th Armored Infantry
Battalion, I am commending a commendation for
Renee Lemaire on the following evidence:

This girl, a registered nurse in the country of Belgium,
volunteered her services at the aid station, 20th
Armored Infantry Battalion in Bastogne, Belgium, 21
December, 1944. At this time the station was holding
about 150 patients since the city was encircled by

enemy forces and evacuation was impossible. Many of these patients were seriously injured and in great need of immediate nursing attention. This girl cheerfully accepted the herculean task and worked without adequate rest or food until the night of her untimely death on 24 December, 1944. She changed dressings, fed patients unable to feed themselves, gave out medications, bathed and made the patients more comfortable, and was of great assistance in the administration of plasma and other professional duties. Her very presence among those wounded men seemed to be an inspiration to those whose morale had declined from prolonged suffering. On the night of December 24 the building in which Renee Lemaire was working was scored with a direct hit by an enemy bomber. She, together with those whom she was caring for so diligently, were instantly killed.

It is on these grounds that I recommend the highest award possible to one, who though not a member of the armed forces of the United States, was of invaluable assistance to us.

Jack T. Prior
Captain, M.C.
Commanding

Renee Bernadette Emilie Lemaire

Place du Carre 30

Bastogne, Belgium

Appendix 9 Other Battle of the Bulge Sites

There are also some other sites not far from Bastogne that are worth visiting if you're interested in seeing more pertaining to the Battle of the Bulge.

Cemeteries

Luxembourg American Cemetery
Web Site:
http://www.abmc.gov/cemeteries/cemeteries/lx.php

Ardennes American Cemetery
Web Site:
http://www.abmc.gov/cemeteries/cemeteries/ar.php

Henri-Chapelle American Cemetery
Web Site:
http://www.abmc.gov/cemeteries/cemeteries/hc.php

Museums

Diekirch National Museum of Military History
Web Site: http://www.mnhm.lu/www/usa/

Musee de la Bataille des Ardennes
Web Site:
http://ardennes.secondworldwar.nl/museums/clervaux.php

Bastogne Ardennes 44 Museum
Web Site: http://www.bastogneardennes44.be

Musee De La Bataille Des Ardennes
Web Site: http://www.batarden.be/

December44 La Gleize Museum
Web Site: http://www.december44.com/

Baugnez 44 Historical Center (Malmedy Massacre)
Web Site: www.baugnez44.be/

Robert R. Allen

Bibliography

Alexander, Larry (2006). Biggest Brother: The Life Of Major Dick Winters, The Man Who Lead The Band Of Brothers. NAL Trade.

Ambrose, Stephen E. (2001). Band Of Brothers: E Company, 506th Regiment, 101st Airborne From Normandy To Hitler's Eagle's Nest. Simon & Schuster.

Anthony C. McAuliffe (n.d.) "Anthony C. McAuliffe". Encyclopedia Britannica Facts Matter. January 11, 2013. From: http://www.britannica.com/EBchecked/topic/3537 46/Anthony-C-McAuliffe.

Arend, Guy F. (1994). Bastogne If You Don't Know What "NUTS" Means. Joh. Enschede.

Brotherton, Marcus. (2010a) We Who Are Alive And Remain: Untold Stories From The Band Of Brothers. Berkley Trade.

Brotherton, Marcus, (2010b). A Company Of Heroes: Personal Memories About The Real Band Of Brothers And The Legacy They Left Us. Berkley Hardcover.

Brotherton, Marcus, (2011). Shifty's War: The Authorized Biography of Sergeant Darrell "Shifty"

Powers, The Legendary Sharpshooter From The Band Of Brothers. Berkley Hardcover.

Chen, C. P. (n.d. a) "Hasso von Manteuffel" World War II Database. January 12, 2013. From: http://ww2db.com/person_bio.php?person_id=131

Chen, C. P. (n.d. b) "Gerd von Rundstedt" World War II Database. January 12, 2013. From: http://ww2db.com/person_bio.php?person_id=29

Cole, Hugh M. (1965). The Ardennes: Battle Of The Bulge. U.S. Government Printing Office.

Collins, Michael & King, Martin (2011). Voices of the Bulge: Untold Stories from Veterans of the Battle of the Bulge. Zenith Press.

Compton, Lynn & Brotherton, Marcus (2009). Call of Duty: My Life Before and After the Band of Brothers. Berkley Trade.

Einhorn, Dalton, (2009). From Toccoa To The Eagle's Nest: Discoveries In The Bootsteps Of The Band Of Brothers. BookSurge Publishing.

George Patton. (n.d.). "George Patton. Biography." Bio.True Story. January 11, 2013. From: http://www.biography.com/people/george-patton-9434904.

Guarnere, William, Heffron, Edward and Post, Robyn (2008). Brothers In Battle, Best Of Friends. Berkley Trade.

Killblane, Richard E. & McNiece, Jake (2003). The Filthy Thirteen: From the Dustbowl to Hitler's Eagle's Nest - The True Story of the 101st Airborne's Most Legendary Squad of Combat Paratroopers. Casemate Publishers and Book Distributors

Killblane, Richard E. (2006). "World War II: Pathfinders Resupply 101st Airborne Division In Bastogne Via Daring Parachute Drop." Weider History Group History net.com Live The History. January 11, 2013. From: http://www.historynet.com/world-war-ii-pathfinders-resupply-101st-airborne-division-troops-in-bastogne-via-daring-parachute-drop.htm.

Koskimaki, George E. (2007). Battered Bastards Of Bastogne The 101st Airborne In The Battle Of The Bulge, December 19, 1944 – January 17, 1945. Presidio Press.

Lüttwitz, Heinrich Freiherr von (n.d.) "Lüttwitz, Heinrich Freiherr von" Lexikon der Wehrmacht. January 11, 2013. From: http://www.lexikon-der-wehrmacht.de/Personenregister/L/LuttwitzHFv-R.htm.

Malarkey, Don and Welch, Bob, (2009). Easy Company Soldier: The Legendary Battles Of A

Sergeant From WWII's "Band Of Brothers". St. Martin's Griffin.

MacDonald, Charles B., (1997). A Time for Trumpets: The Untold Story of the Battle of the Bulge. William Morrow Paperbacks.

McManus, John C., (2008). Alamo in the Ardennes: The Untold Story of the American Soldiers Who Made the Defense of Bastogne Possible. NAL Trade.

Mundt, Joel, (n.d.). Montgomery Weighs In On The Bulge. "Today's History Lesson Bringing Yesterday's Headlines To Today's Readers". January 11, 2013. From:
http://todayshistorylesson.wordpress.com/2010/01/07/montgomery-weighs-in-on-the-bulge/.

Toland, John and D'Este, Carlo, (1999). Battle: The Story Of The Bulge. Bison Books.

von Lauchert (n.d.). "von Lauchert, Meienrad" Lexikon der Wehrmacht. January 11, 2013. From: http://www.lexikon-der-wehrmacht.de/Personenregister/L/LauchertM-R.htm

Webster, David K., (2008). Parachute Infantry: An American Paratrooper's Memoir Of D-Day And The Fall Of The Third Rich. Dell.

Winters, Dick and Kingseed, Cole C., (2006). Beyond The Band Of Brothers: The War Memoirs Of Major Dick Winters. Berkley Hardcover..

Index

ABOUT THE AUTHOR

Bob Allen is a graduate of University of Maryland University College with a minor in history. He is a member of the Alpha Epsilon Chi chapter of the Phi Alpha Theta History Honor Society. He currently works part time for the Kaiserslautern USO as a military history tour guide. He has been in Germany for 22 years and has traveled extensively to the battlefield sites to study the events where they happened.

Lightning Source UK Ltd.
Milton Keynes UK
UKOW06f1437160316

270280UK00002B/57/P